Ordinary Time

A Journey of Counting,
Conforming and Embracing
God's Presence in Everyday Life

By Erik E. Willits

ORDINARY TIME:
A Journey of Counting, Conforming and
Embracing God's Presence in Everyday Life

Copyright © 2015 by Erik E. Willits
Publisher: Mark Oestreicher
Managing Editor: Tamara Rice
Cover Design: Adam McLane
Layout: Marilee R. Pankratz
Creative Director: Rosemary N. Thyme

ISBN-10: 1942145101
ISBN-13: 978-1-942145-10-3

The Youth Cartel, LLC
www.theyouthcartel.com
Email: info@theyouthcartel.com
Born in San Diego
Printed in the U.S.A.

Table of Contents

Welcome to a Journey of Discovery – page 3

How to Use This Book – page 5

Ordinary Time Web Guide – page 7

THREE [Days 1-7] – page 9

GROW [Days 8-14] – page 17

IMAGINE [Days 15-21] – page 25

STORY [Days 22-28] – page 33

FAITH [Days 29-35] – page 41

LOVE [Days 36-42] – page 49

VIRTUE [Days 43-49] – page 57

FEAR [Days 50-56] – page 65

EXAMEN [Days 57-63] – page 73

REAL [Days 64-70] – page 81

NOW [Days 71-77] – page 89

FOLLOW [Days 78-84] – page 97

POINTING [Days 85-91] – page 105

To my community of friends and family, especially the folks at
Christ Church Plano. Thanks for loving me and my crew.
To my crew, Andrea, Jack, Reese and Soren—let's keep dancing!

Welcome to a Journey of Discovery

Ordinary Time is the period of weeks and months that follow the celebratory seasons of Christmas and Easter, as well as the more intense seasons of spiritual preparation like Advent and Lent on what we call the liturgical calendar. This liturgical calendar is the way we keep time with the Church and not just the culture. While you can start this journey at any time, it was written to start with Trinity Sunday, which is the fifth Sunday after Easter. The "ordinary" in Ordinary Time comes from the word *ordinal*, as in the ordinal numbers—like first, second and third. This is the case because nothing very exciting is happening during this time of the year, so we simply count the Sundays after Pentecost leading up to Advent, which is the season that kicks off the liturgical year. So if Ordinary Time is simply about counting the weeks of the year when nothing is happening, what exactly will we discover on this journey?

Let me explain it this way. If it was your birthday every day, would you love it? I'm sure your impulse is to say you would, but if you really think about it, you would probably change your mind. Part of what makes a birthday or holiday so great is the space "in between"—the build-up, the anticipation, the time you're given to decide what you really want. My five-year-old son enjoys the 364 days a year that aren't his birthday because he has time to ask for anything and everything he wants—just go to the store with him. This builds his anticipation in such a way that his birthday and Christmas are like the best days ever. There is a beauty in the space between, a truth in the mundane, a candor to the boring and a purpose for the ordinary.

The Church offers similar rhythms. We have all the familiar feasts and festivals; important days when we celebrate and remember and retell events like the birth of Jesus (Christmas), his resurrection (Easter) and the birth of the Church (Pentecost). Throughout the year, we may also participate in a handful of lesser-known feast days like All Saints Day, Trinity Sunday, The Annunciation and more. But in the Church calendar, there is also a pretty large chunk of time that we, the Church, call ordinary. Ordinary Time is the space "in between" that helps us be shaped and formed by the life of Christ in everyday, ordinary ways.

In her book *The Liturgical Year*, Joan Chittister highlights that part of the reason for this delineation of time was so that people would feel the weight and importance of the two primary feast days for the Church: Christmas and Easter. So instead of packing the calendar with dates and memorials of the works of Jesus and his followers, we keep a pretty long season of the year simple, plain ... ordinary. When a large portion of the year is ordinary, the peaks seem higher and the deserts seem dryer.

I remember moving to Colorado after a couple years of grad school. I needed a break and I needed to be refreshed. As I drove through Kansas and Nebraska, I thought, *Wow, this is flat and plain—not much is happening here.* It kind of reflected my inner life and the season I had been living in for the several years prior. As I approached Colorado, I began to see the Rocky Mountains in the distance and my anticipation started to build. When the mountains came into clear view, they seemed so exciting, so glorious! When I finally reached the summit and made my home in the "resurrection" mountains of Vail, Colorado, it felt like exactly what I needed, exactly where I was supposed to be. No doubt the splendor and beauty of that geography was heightened because of the very long stretch of ordinary, flat land I had just experienced.

It may be plain and flat, but Ordinary Time is also a green season for Christians. In addition to the flourishing foliage of summer that you might see around, we also see the liturgical color green used for vestments and hangings inside many churches during this time of year. That's because Ordinary Time is marked by growth, maturing and blooming after seasons of tilling the soil and extravagant spiritual outpouring— seasons like Advent and Lent and then Christmas, Easter and Pentecost. During Ordinary Time, we see the natural, ordinary, everyday growth that results from living through dry, difficult, pruning seasons as well as seasons of abundant, water-soaked, sun-drenched celebration and Spirit-empowerment. During Ordinary Time, we simply let the fruit that the rest of the year plants in us come to maturity. We let our extraordinary encounters with God enable us to live faithful, ordinary lives in ordinary times.

So welcome to Ordinary Time. Rest. Settle in. Grow. Bear fruit. Get bored. Feel blah. Count the days. Enjoy the plains. Anticipate the mountains. Be present. It's okay. Walk—don't run. Take a breath. Learn the rhythms of abundant life. Let the Spirit teach you how to follow Jesus in Nebraska, not just in Vail or Death Valley. Life is, more often than not, simply ordinary. Let's discover how to live here—it's Ordinary Time.

How to Use This Book ...

Ordinary Time lasts all summer long and leads up to Advent. That's about a 26-week stretch of time. This book will guide you through about half of that and really it's created for the first half of Ordinary Time, but you can pick it up whenever you want to start the journey. I would recommend that you get a group of friends together or gather your church or youth group and take the summer, go through these day together, think and pray about what ordinary means for those who follow Jesus.

You'll find that each day is comprised of Scripture readings, reflections and meditations as well as questions for every day of the journey. The Scripture verses themselves have been intentionally left out of this book so that you can engage with the passages in your own Bible. Highlight the verses, take notes, doodle ... use the physical pages in your Bible as part of the journey. It may be easy to skip over this part and head straight into the devotion, but I encourage you to take the extra minute or two, sit down with your Bible and read the Scripture for the day. If you only do one thing, do this.

After the Scripture, you'll find a brief devotional thought and sometimes a meditation from a writer, scholar, thinker or interesting person. All of this will help you think more deeply about that week's theme. Some days the reading may be challenging—with some big theological words or maybe some ideas you haven't thought about before—but don't be discouraged. If you don't understand something, ask someone in your community (a parent, friend or pastor) or you can even email me (my information is included in the back of the book). I would love to listen to your questions and help you find answers.

On Sundays, you will find four Scripture readings from the Revised Common Lectionary, which is a list of specific verses to be used each Sunday from the first of the year all the way through the end—something many churches all over the world use to plan their worship services. Reading the same Scriptures as thousands of other Christians around the globe helps us remember that we are a part of something amazing and big. We are not alone on this journey.

Now Ordinary Time has a lot of nuances to it. Like the English language, depending on how you use, read and encounter letters, words and spaces, sometimes the exact same compilation of characters can evoke a very different response and interaction. This book will lead you to engage Ordinary Time in a couple different ways.

1. Seeing God's Presence in the Everyday

Ordinary Time shows us the reality that most of the time, life is ordinary. In the Christian life, though, we often seek out the extraordinary. We can't wait for the next big conference, camp, retreat or even the next big church service where we will "connect with Jesus" and experience this extraordinary God. Wanting the extraordinary in our lives is a good and natural impulse. We are loved and we belong to an extraordinary God! The danger lies in our desire to jump from event to event, church service to church service, forgetting to focus on living every day in and with the presence of God—here and now, not just "someday" or Sunday. As we worship week after week, we remember the risen and reigning Christ is present, at all times and in all places. When life is boring, tragic or spectacular, he is present and guiding us.

2. Living the Ordinary Well

For those of us who desire to follow Jesus and continually become more like him, I hope we can begin to view Ordinary Time as an opportunity to learn to live the ordinary life well. Have you ever heard the phrase "a new normal"? In Ordinary Time, we are learning to live a "new ordinary." The ordinary life of a Christian is often extraordinary to those around us because the life Jesus calls us to live—the daily, faithful, living and breathing, working and resting, walking and waiting life modeled by the teachings and the life of Jesus—is anything but ordinary in our culture. We look like aliens in this strange land. So Ordinary Time is a space to learn how to live this extraordinary life Jesus calls and teaches us to live in everyday ways that will, with time, become our ordinary way of life as it was his.

The Ordinary Time Web Guide is a supplement to this book. There, you will find images and icons, videos, more great meditative quotes and Bible readings, as well as an opportunity to leave comments, ask questions and share a bit of your journey through this Ordinary Time.

www.OrdinaryTimeWebGuide.com

As you're reading, look for these icons.

SNAP!
There's a picture, image or Christian icon
for you to check out!

You're only a click away.
We've posted a link to a website, blog or
something cool for you to look at!

We've got a great video, YouTube,
Vimeo or other goodie for you to watch.

Listen up!
We've posted an audio clip, sermon
or message for you to listen to!

We like the Bible around here!
When you see this, we've got more
Scripture for you!

Get ready to be inspired!
We've posted a quote or meditation
that you won't want to miss.

There's an app for that.
We've provided a link to an app for your smart
phone that might help you on this journey.

It's time to experiment!
Get ready to experiment with living
out what you're learning!

THREE

ORDINARY TIME :: SUNDAY #1
TRINITY SUNDAY*

Isaiah 6:1-8	Romans 8:12-17
Psalm 29	John 3:1-17

* While these Scriptures are meant to be read on Trinity Sunday (the fifth Sunday after Easter or, if your church celebrates Pentecost, the Sunday after Pentecost), you can start your journey through Ordinary Time on any Sunday you like.

It makes sense to start off our first week of Ordinary Time with a simple, ordinary number: THREE. The Trinity, God as Three-in-One, is anything but ordinary, but it just so happens that the first Sunday of Ordinary Time is what the church calls Trinity Sunday, when we celebrate the Triune God. This belief in God as Three-in-One, as a divine community of persons—Father, Son and Holy Spirit—is actually the best way for us to frame this entire journey through Ordinary Time, so let's dig in.

If you're interested in growing your faith, it's because on some level you want what God wants for you, right? Or at least you want to want what God wants. The cool thing about God is that he has shown us what he wants in God's triune self, in who he is.

God the Father. God shows us his desire for intimacy, for the all-consuming closeness a parent hopes to always experience with their child. We find a constant and unconditional love and relationship in God the Father.

God the Son. God shows his own heart with flesh and blood on it and gives us the ultimate example to follow in the person of Jesus.

The Holy Spirit. God shows his desire to enable, transform and lead us with God's ever-present, empowering self. We are filled and begin to drip with his divine life, this growth we call the fruit of the Spirit.

God is always giving; giving himself as Father, Son and Holy Spirit. He gives himself to us as a means to rescue us, lead us and grow us more and more into his image and likeness for the good of the world. Plain and simple, God is always giving himself to us as an act of love. Believe that, and let it shape and guide you!

Have you ever thought about how the Trinity is relevant to your everyday, ordinary life? Head over to the Web Guide for six reflective experiences with the Trinity in everyday life.

God: A Divine Community of Persons.

Do you ever wonder why you long for relationship and community? Why you want more than anything to love and be loved? Why you desire so deeply to be listened to and even just to be in the presence of another person who is fully present to you?

This desire is deep in your bones because you were created in the image and likeness of God. You were created to reflect your Creator who is always in community. God is a mysterious and divine community of persons, Three-in-One: Father, Son and Holy Spirit.

Now let's be honest. We don't get it, and when it comes to God, when it comes to the Trinity, I might suggest that it is okay. I've heard a St. Augustine quote along the lines of, "If you can understand it, then it is not God." It's a reminder that we'd be well served to remember from time to time that God is bigger then our minds and imaginations, and that is a truly good thing.

We use a lot of analogies and metaphors that attempt to help us wrap our minds around the Trinity. But if we were honest, they all fall short. The simplest and, I think, most formative aspect of the Trinity is the idea that God is a community in and of God's self. This is often referred to as the divine community of persons.

Think about it this way. Because God is love (1 John 4:8), there has to be a relationship there. Right? In order for there to be love, there must be an object of that love—a lover and a beloved. Love cannot exist outside a relationship, and Scripture tells us that GOD IS LOVE. If we are created in the image and likeness of God, that means we are created for community, to be connected to God and to one another. We were not created to live life alone.

As we begin this journey through the season of Ordinary Time—a time to simply live and breathe, counting the simple, ordinary days of our lives—ask yourself, who am I taking this journey with?

God :: The Father

Meditation ::.

"Some people see God as a transcendent deity who is disconnected from the real world and not involved in people's lives. Others think God is waiting around to strike them with a lightning bolt every time they do something wrong. The truth is God is our Father and we are his children ... The fact that God is our heavenly Father is foundational to the Christian faith. Everything else flows from this great truth. Jesus said, 'As the Father has loved me, so have I loved you' (John 15:9) ... The Fatherhood of God is an amazing spiritual reality that is both humbling and life-changing. God loves poor and lost sinners as a father loves his children. God loves you and me more than we can imagine or will ever know. If we never learned anything else about God, this would be enough."

— from *Creed* by Winfield Bevins
(from a section titled "Who's Your Daddy?")

It's no accident that Jesus starts off his most formative and instructive prayer with, "Our Father ..." Jesus is inviting us all to know and relate to God in this close and personal way. But for many people, including myself, it's hard to connect with God on this level. I grew up without a father involved in my life. When I heard God was referred to as a father, I wasn't sure I wanted anything to do with that. Many of us have had broken, destructive or nonexistent relationships with our fathers, and we superimpose what we know about fathers onto our Heavenly Father.

But go ahead and bring to mind the best dad you know—he doesn't have to be your own. Then make a list of the attributes that make this dad so awesome. Prayerfully engage this list and know that God is perfectly all of these things to you and for you!

How has your earthly dad shaped your vision of your Heavenly Father?
How might God want to expand your perspective today?

God :: The Son

Meditation ::.

"We are at all times to '[look to] Jesus, the founder and perfecter of our faith' (Hebrews12:2). But we are to look to him in a way that lets us see him situated in his relationships to the Father who sent him and the Spirit whom he sends. Unless we see Jesus in this way, we fail to see him as who he actually is."

— from *The Deep Things of God* by Fred Sanders

The entire season of Ordinary Time could be spent looking at the life of Jesus. Jesus shows us definitively what ordinary looks like in the Kingdom of God. What he did and how he did it, who he loved and how he loved them—his life was one perfect snapshot of how humanity was meant to live in fullness and alignment with God and his Kingdom.

If you could take away all the complexity, layers and difficulty of daily following Jesus and simply stick with him, get covered in his dust and do nothing else but walk around with him, soaking up his example, you would be sticking with the Father and the Spirit as well. If you were to simply follow Jesus, you would be obsessed with doing what the Father was doing (John 5:19-20) and being led by the Spirit (Luke 4:1-2).

At the core of who he is and what he came to do, Jesus shows us how to live in relationship to God, our neighbor and our world. He teaches us how to do the will of the Father and be led by the Holy Spirit. He is the example of how to be authentically human in an often dehumanizing world. We follow him, imitate him, embrace his attitudes and virtues. Jesus teaches us how to live—every day, all of our days—the abundant, eternal life we were created for. Jesus says, "I have come that they may have life, and have it to the full" (John 10:10).

Follow Jesus through one of the Gospels today (Matthew, Mark, Luke or John). Ask yourself while reading how you might better follow Jesus in this full, abundant life of the Kingdom?

God :: The Holy Spirit

Meditation ::.

> "The Spirit is not man's own potential, but entirely the gift, the power
> and strength of God."
> — from *The Church* by Hans Küng

Have you ever wished you could drink a special drink or eat a magical food that would enable you to jump higher, shoot better, get straight A's or just be plain awesome? Yeah, me too. I might propose this is why superhero movies are huge these days, and energy drinks sell millions every year. We love the idea of a magic pill or an extra boost.

Many people think that's how the Holy Spirit works. We say things like, "If I can just get filled with the Spirit," and there's nothing wrong with that, but often the Holy Spirit winds up being treated like our spiritual energy drink that can turn us into the Christian superheroes we think we're supposed to be. However, I'm not sure this thinking leads to the kind of radically ordinary lives we were created to live.

In Acts Chapter 8, Simon the Sorcerer wanted what the disciples had so he could do what they were doing. This guy wanted the magic pill or power drink, making it obvious his heart was not in the right place (verse 21). He didn't get what he wanted because that's not how the Spirit works. The Spirit is not for show, not to be earned or paid for.

Rather, the Spirit is the infilling of God, gifted to you, so you can actually live the life you were created to live, in the image and likeness of God as seen in Christ. Scripture even says the Holy Spirit is the "power of God" (Romans 15:13). This isn't a superhero kind of power; it's a Kingdom living kind of power, enabling us to live in obedience to the Father, in the example of the Son, in peace-filled community with each other.

What evidence or fruit do you see in your life that the Spirit fills you?
Who can you give that fruit to today?

Meditation ::.

"To have the 'right' answer about the Trinity, for example, and to actually believe in the reality of the Trinity, is all the difference in the world.

The advantage of believing in the reality of the Trinity is not that we get an A from God for giving 'the right answer.' Remember, to believe something is to act as if it is so. To believe that two plus two equals four is to behave accordingly when trying to find out how many dollars or apples are in the house. The advantage of believing it is not that we can pass tests in arithmetic; it is that we can deal much more successfully with reality. Just try dealing with it as if two plus two equals six.

Hence, the advantage of believing in the Trinity is that we then live as if the Trinity is real: as if the cosmos envisioning us actually is, beyond all else, a self-sufficing community of unspeakably magnificent personal beings of boundless love, knowledge and power. And, thus believing, our lives naturally integrate themselves, through our actions, into the reality of such a universe, just as with two plus two equals four. In faith we rest ourselves upon the reality of the Trinity in action—and it graciously meets us. For it is there. And our lives are then enmeshed in the true world of God."

— from *The Divine Conspiracy* by Dallas Willard

We begin this journey of Ordinary Time realizing that in Christ we have life and are given relationship with the Father and empowerment by the Spirit. We rest in God, Father, Son and Holy Spirit, knowing that embracing and believing in the Triune God will help us, in the end, to navigate this crazy world. So we continue to learn to love him, follow him and be led by him—Father, Son and Holy Spirit—through all the ordinary days of our lives.

What has been the most significant and inspiring aspect of thinking about the Trinity this week? How might you carry these ideas with you for the next twelve weeks of Ordinary Time?

GROW

ORDINARY TIME :: SUNDAY #2

1 Samuel 8:4-20; 11:14-15	2 Corinthians 4:13-5:1
Psalm 138	Mark 3:20-35

Look around. I mean, really look. Is there anything in your line of vision that is growing? Let me answer that for you—yes!

Growth is always happening all around us. During Ordinary Time we remember that growth should be a normal occurrence not only around us in nature, but in us as well. Even in the mundane, ordinary, day-in-day-out moments of life, those who are connected to Christ should be growing.

Each season creates a particular climate for growth. During the spring, we plant and see things come alive. During the summer, we see those things mature and flourish. In the fall, we harvest that growth. Then in winter, everything dies and the land lays bare, waiting for the cycle of life to come back around. And the Church year or liturgical year offers similar climates for growth in the Christian life. Advent is for waiting and wanting, Christmas is for feasting and celebrating, Lent is for fasting and self-denying preparation, Easter is for resurrection and new life and Ordinary Time is for growth, fruit and learning the new normal for the Christian life in the Kingdom of God.

Meditation ::.

"It is you and God, down on the farm. You have entered, I do believe, into a holy equation that depends on sun and rain and soil. Too much, too little, and all is lost. Days and weeks and months of labor, of getting up at dawn, of sweat rolling down your nose and muscles aching. Of praying. On your knees begging for rain close to come on, to bring the benediction that just might be a quarter inch of rain. It is, I do believe, a hands-on PhD in all the truths of life. Birth and death and resurrection, sometimes. Anticipation. Heartbreak. Hallelujahs."

— from *Slowing Time: Seeing the Sacred Outside Your Kitchen Door*
by Barbara Mahany

Are you ready to begin this journey
through a season of ordinary growth?

Nothing is more important to growth than the sun. Have you ever seen a flower literally growing in the direction of the sun, as if reaching its entire life toward what it wants and needs the most? I've always thought it was crazy that a plant could know enough to grow toward the source of its life.

A few years ago I was able to spend a couple of weeks in Alaska. I was fortunate to visit during the summertime! Alaska in the summer is beautiful, sunny, green, teeming with life. Part of the reason for the beauty and growth is the light—bright, shining sunlight pouring down for the entire day. At one point in the summer, the sun shines 24 hours a day.

I remember being awake at two in the morning, sitting on the back patio of my cabin, reading a book. I didn't need a lamp because the sun was still bright overhead. But the opposite is true as well. There is a day in the winter when Alaskans experience 24 hours of darkness. I was told that the winter months can be pretty tough—not only because of the extreme cold but because of the lack of sunshine.

We are all fruit-bearing, living creatures. Like plants, we human beings need the sun to live. Many of my friends in Alaska have special light bulbs in their homes or go to tanning beds in the winter to give their bodies what they are missing from the sun. They know they can't grow and thrive if they don't have frequent time in the light.

It's obvious there are spiritual implications of this truth we witness in life and nature. We are all living, breathing, spiritual selves who need the Son. We can't grow or become who we were created to be unless we regularly sit in the Son, rest in the Son, are with the Son. Our hearts and souls desire so deeply to be connected to Jesus that when we take the time to daily sit with him, our lives begin to bend in his direction and likeness. The growth is evident in a person who exposes herself or himself regularly to Jesus.

You may include Bible studies, community groups or church services in your plan for spiritual growth, but how much time are you allowing to simply just sit in the Son? Let Jesus shine his life-giving light into your thirsty soul.

WEDNESDAY // DAY 11
READING :: 1 Corinthians 13:8-13

Growth happens in many areas of our lives. As people, we are expected to grow emotionally, mentally and spiritually. If we find that a person isn't growing in all these expected ways, we eventually take some kind of action to stimulate the growth.

Imagine a six-month-old baby standing up in his crib, hopping over the rail, lowering himself down and walking to the bathroom, where he takes off his diaper, lifts up the toilet seat and proceeds to do his business.

It's unbelievable, right? Babies are supposed to use their diapers, if you know what I mean. Babies are supposed to do baby things. As they grow and mature, they learn to walk—usually around twelve to fifteen months, in case you were wondering—and use the bathroom and sleep in a regular bed. All these things happen at the right time as a child grows and matures.

Now, if a high school student was still wearing a diaper and sleeping in a crib, we would know there was a developmental problem, to say the least. As a teenager, you're supposed to be past these things.

The Scriptures talk a lot about growth and maturity in our spiritual lives. The Apostle Paul describes people and, by extension, churches who are not growing like they are supposed to. In our reading for today, he makes this point very clear.

We all are called to grow and mature into love and all the facets of love that Paul lists in 1 Corinthians. God is love, and in him we see perfectly all of the actions listed in this passage. As we mature in our relationship with God, we will grow in love and reflect him more and more.

Are you and the people you share life with seeing and experiencing this maturity God is bringing about in your life? Or are you still acting and talking like children? Would others say you are growing into the mature, Christ-following, God-reflecting person you were created to be?

When we think of growth, it's natural to think of getting bigger, stronger and smarter. We also assume certain things go along with those attributes, things like power, money, success. In our world, a leader is defined as one who has the most power, strength, success and money. This often results in "leaders" being pretty poor examples or just plain jerks.

In the Kingdom of God—that place where God rules and reigns and where we seek to live as citizens, people who follow King Jesus—leaders are those who have experienced growth and are maturing. The Kingdom of God is "upside down" in comparison to the kingdoms we see around us in our world, so growth and maturity for the follower of Jesus doesn't necessarily equate to power and strength, but rather humility and service. We find generosity and meekness along the way of maturity, instead of riches and persuasive words. The mature follower of Jesus is continually learning to look not to his or her own interests but rather to the interest of others (Philippians 2:4). Rather than power and autonomy, this growth leads to submission and community.

Meditation ::.

"Jesus has a different vision of maturity: It is the ability and willingness to be led where you would rather not go. Immediately after Peter has been commissioned to be a leader of his sheep, Jesus confronts him with the hard truth that the servant-leader is the leader who is being led to unknown, undesirable and painful places. The way of the Christian leader is not the way of upward mobility in which our world invests so much, but the way of downward mobility ending on the cross."

— from *In the Name of Jesus* by Henri Nouwen

What are your goals when it comes to growth, maturity and leadership? Do they reflect the Scriptures and the life of Jesus? Are they for the sake of your neighbor and the glory of God, or are they primarily about your advancement and agenda? How might you step onto the path of Jesus and follow him into maturity as an authentically Christian (Christlike) person and leader?

In our Scripture today, the Apostle Paul tells us that he's not perfect (see verse twelve). Instead, he's on a journey, running a race. His journey is one of chasing after Jesus, the one who has pursued and taken hold of Paul. Paul's goal—the perfection he seeks but hasn't achieved—is to embrace and know Christ with every fiber of his being. Paul wants to be connected to Christ and his resurrection power. Then in verse fifteen Paul says, "All of us, then, who are mature should take such a view of things. And if at some point you think differently, that too God will make clear to you."

Some people think this statement lacks a bit of humility. I think it's kind of funny. He's essentially saying, "If you don't agree with me, no worries. God will change your mind eventually." Now that's confidence! But I want to focus on what maturity means here, specifically the Greek word *telios*, which we translate to "mature."

Telios can also be translated as "perfect." As in perfectly obedient, receiving God's will with a yes—a surrender-filled, obedient-hearted yes. So this kind of maturity is about living what you know to be true and good. It's about being obedient in heart, mind and action to the one you serve and study under.

But you'll notice a few verses earlier Paul says, "Not that I have already obtained this or am already **perfect**" (ESV). The Greek word for perfect in this verse, *telioo*, is similar, but miles apart in definition. Paul's original audience, the hearers of this letter, would have picked up on this nuance. *Telioo* is like the perfection of a puzzle once you have moved that last piece into place. Nothing can be (or needs to be) added. Everything is exactly as it should be: Complete! Perfect! And Paul says, "I'm not there yet."

Our goal as Christians is to be obedient, always saying yes and moving deeper into the embrace of Jesus. Maturity is a journey for us as it is for Paul. We are all on a journey toward living in deeper obedience to the Father and with an ever-increasing likeness to the Son. That sounds "perfect" to me!

How do Paul's words help us understand what it means to live the obedient, Jesus-following life we're created to live?

There is an intentionality to growth. It's not just going to happen. Any kind of growth takes the intention of the one who is doing the growing. Whether they are growing an external seed or the personal, internal seeds of the Kingdom, the one who grows must put his or her heart, soul, mind and strength to the plow. I'm confident this is why Jesus says this is the most important of the commandments: "Love the Lord your God with all your heart, soul, mind and strength" (Mark 12:30). I believe this is why Paul talks so radically about not conforming but renovating our minds (Romans 12:2). I am also pretty sure this is why we see so little spiritual growth in our own lives and communities. It's hard work being a gardener and maybe even harder work being the garden.

As the gardener, you can fertilize, water, give shade or sun, protect from bugs and vermin, till soil, prune leaves and pull weeds. You can do it all and maybe, just maybe, you'll experience the growth you want. In our spiritual lives, our efforts don't necessarily cause the growth either. They are simply faithful ways to give God the readied soil to do what he, our constant gardener, does: cause the growth. There may be some correlation between our efforts and the fruit that grows in our lives, but the gardening efforts of our inner lives don't necessarily cause the growth. That's God's domain, and his alone.

The tricky thing about this metaphor is that you are not only the gardener in participation with God. You are also the very fruit-bearing garden that is being grown. As the garden, you must simply be and have faith that the God who causes the sun to shine and the rain to fall will bring about the growth he desires as he desires it.

This may be why the words *grace* and *growth* go so well together and should become part of our everyday, ordinary vocabulary as gardeners and gardens, producing fruit for the good of those who cross our paths each day.

How are you working the soil of your inner life? What disciplines and rhythms are you practicing? And do you take time to simply be the garden, ripe and ready for God to cause growth?

IMAGINE

ORDINARY TIME :: SUNDAY #3

1 Samuel 15:34-16:13	2 Corinthians 5:6-17
Psalm 20	Mark 4:26-34

MONDAY // DAY 16
READING :: Romans 8:1-16

Meditation ::.

Almighty and eternal God, so draw our hearts to you, so guide our minds, so fill our imaginations, so control our wills, that we may be wholly yours, utterly dedicated unto you; and then use us, we pray, as you will, and always to the glory and the welfare of your people; through our Lord and Savior Jesus Christ. Amen.

— from "A Prayer of Self-Dedication" in *The Book of Common Prayer*

At my church, we pray this prayer every Tuesday at our noon Eucharist service. This week, let's use this prayer as a daily center and guide as we ponder the way in which God, through his self-giving love and infilling Spirit, guides our minds and fills our imaginations.

If we seek to draw close to our Father, look more like his Son and be led by his Spirit, this prayer might just help us go further down that road in loving and serving all those who cross our path.

Do you have a time every day you commit to prayer and sitting in God's presence?
Add this prayer to your daily rhythm with God.

I've been told my imagination is "overly active." I am always constructing potential scenarios about my life, relationships and decisions that need to be made. It's like living a constant "choose your own adventure" book. Sometimes this is fun and sometimes I wish I could just turn it off.

A few months ago, I attended a silent retreat and was able to sit down with a Jesuit priest for some spiritual direction. After about an hour I was ready to get some of the built-up thoughts out of my ready-to-bust brain. I told the priest I had a hard time just being silent, listening to God and quieting my mind and imagination. I even mentioned that I was living with ADHD. It wasn't serious, I would live, but often I wasn't sure if my prayer life would make it. He smiled at me and, to my surprise, told me I was lucky. He said that my ADHD could be a strength rather than a detriment. The priest encouraged me to invite God into every random, wandering thought in my mind and to trust that the very Spirit of God was at work. Maybe some of those thoughts I believed to be random were the very things God was trying to talk to me about.

Often we want to guide our own minds and fill our own imaginations. But remember, our prayer for this week is that God would do the guiding and filling. So we offer our minds and imaginations up to God in obedience, giving every thing and every thought over to Christ. We trust that he is doing what we ask him. Challenge yourself to draw close to the Father as Jesus, through the Spirit, fills your imagination with the very things he wants to share with you.

Are you ready to invite God into your thoughts—each and every one?

Just about everybody loves C. S. Lewis. He was a theologian and an apologist who wrote deeply profound books about life, faith and God. *Mere Christianity* is one of his best-known theological works. The case for Christianity that he sets forth in that book has influenced just about every corner of the Church and Christian culture.

Now, you probably know him as the author of *The Lion, the Witch and the Wardrobe*, but when I first found out that C. S. Lewis, this deep and profound theologian, also wrote novels like that about talking animals and a parallel dimension kids get to through a magic wardrobe, I was baffled. In my mind, you either wrote deep theological words or you told good stories in novels—somehow C. S. Lewis did both.

Lewis knew something I have since come to understand: Our imaginations are powerful tools when it comes to shaping our hearts and minds. Lewis understood that the stories we read shape the imaginations we have and prompt the lives we live.

Fr. Robert Barron says, "C. S. Lewis was primarily an evangelist of the imagination." Perhaps more of us need to embrace that form of evangelism, living and telling such compelling stories of Jesus and his Kingdom that people will be drawn into the amazing gospel narrative.

Christians are fortunate—we have the best story ever told at our fingertips. It's the story of God and creation, of Jesus and redemption and of the Spirit and abundant life. We forget from time to time and try to coerce and argue people into the Kingdom of heaven; but at our best, Christians have told this compelling story of God's creative love in ways that have shaped the imaginations of millions and influenced culture everywhere.

Have you ever shared a compelling or dramatic story with a friend?
In the same way, how can you appeal to a person's imagination when sharing God's story?

29

Meditation ::.

"Our inner life is like a banana tree filled with monkeys jumping up and down. It is not easy to sit and trust that in solitude God will speak—not as a magical voice but as a knowledge that grows gradually over the years. And in that word from God we will find the inner place from which to live our lives. Solitude is where Jesus listened to God. It is where we listen to God. Solitude is where community begins."

— from *A Spirituality of Living* by Henri Nouwen

Henri Nouwen's words resonate deeply for me because, as I've said, I have a hard time keeping my "mind monkeys" from completely taking over. I realize my only hope for an ordered inner life and mind is through the help of the Spirit.

Nouwen also says in his book, "It takes real discipline to let God and not the world be the Lord of our mind." Because contemplation isn't a natural bent in my life, I'm not the kind of guy who can go into the woods for days at a time with nothing but my own thoughts and come out refreshed and ready to take on the world. But I took a spiritual temperament test on a work retreat this past year, and one of my top two temperaments was "contemplative." Wow! This shows me God is working in my life. I'm not sure that test would have looked remotely similar a few years ago.

It's exciting to think that with God's help, my spiritual director's help and some good and godly relationships, I am experiencing significant growth that only the Spirit of God can bring about. I am learning to herd my monkeys and order my desires rightly around Jesus and the life he desires to live in and through me. I have light-years to go, I am still totally and completely a novice, but I'm on the path and for this ADHD kid, that is a really big deal.

Are you on the path to a well-ordered inner life? Ask God to empower you to quiet your mind and listen for him to speak to you.

Letting God fill our imagination is a deeply faithful activity in the life of the Jesus-follower. Imagining connects us to hope and the future but also to everyday life.

Professor and author Walter Brueggemann penned an amazing book called *The Prophetic Imagination*. He says that we live in a world filled with imaginations stirred by the dominant culture and the prevailing powers of the time. Brueggemann uses the term "royal consciousness" as he explains that the kingdoms we reside in—our country, family, schools, etc.—all tell us stories about life, what can and can't be done and what makes for a productive, desirable existence. The narratives of our culture shape our actions and desires.

Brueggemann argues that we must have prophetic imaginations. Imaginations that are stirred by the narrative of Jesus who was crucified and three days later rose from the dead. His vision for our lives that you've just read in his Sermon on the Mount and his supernatural story set our imaginations on fire. In fact, the Bible is full of people living and telling a better story, offering an alternative narrative to anyone willing to listen and follow the one true God.

Brueggemann says, "It is the vocation of the prophet to keep alive the ministry of imagination, to keep on conjuring and proposing futures alternative to the single one the king wants to urge as the only thinkable one."

During Ordinary Time we have a bit of extra space to be this kind of prophet—dreaming and imagining based on the incredible events we've just experienced during Advent, Christmas, Lent and Easter. Can you imagine the plans God is unfolding in our world today and in your own life? This faithful activity of imagining should be a normal part of all our lives.

What do you want to do with your life? Why did you choose these goals? Spend some time today evaluating how your goals might change if you allowed God to inspire your imagination.

Have you ever tried to imagine a better world—one with no war, no disease or even sickness? Maybe when you imagine this ideal world, you think of families being united, friendships being mutual, consistent and trustworthy. Maybe there is no death, poverty, addiction, homelessness, sex trafficking, hunger or disparity of any kind.

Now here's the thing: Why isn't the world you live in like that? Is your reflex to say, "Because of sin, of course"? Do you blame Satan or maybe even God because he isn't acting quickly and decisively enough? What if the blame lay more squarely on you than any of the previously mentioned scapegoats? Now that's a sobering thought.

The blame doesn't rest on any one person, however, but on the entire Church. For hundreds of years we, the Church, have often contributed to earth being more like hell than heaven. There is no doubt about that.

Our minds and imaginations, as individuals and as a community, come with a responsibility. When we use our imaginations to escape the dominant narratives of consumerism and self-preservation, of wealth and upward mobility, things begin to change.

Do you imagine a world free of addiction? Maybe your calling is to serve addicts. Can you imagine a world free of slavery? Your mission might be wrapped up in freeing men and women bound by sex traffickers. When you can imagine a world where the poor are blessed, parties are the norm, feasting is experienced by all, and death only leads to life, then you are called to bring those bits of heaven to earth, to your "now." You are called to share the Kingdom of God, the pieces of "already" despite there being so much "not yet."

Your imagination is a responsibility! You are called, like Solomon serve God with wholehearted devotion and with a willing mind and imagination.

What has God stirred in your heart and mind? Has an image, person or problem continued to come to mind? How might you bring your Spirit-led imagination to life for the sake of those who need a taste of heaven?

STORY

ORDINARY TIME :: SUNDAY #4

1 Samuel 17:1, 4-11, 19 & 32-49
Psalm 9:9-20

2 Corinthians 6:1-13
Mark 4:35-41

So a good and compelling story is a really big deal. Did you check out the Web Guide last week and watch the video reflections on the life of C. S. Lewis? In it, Fr. Robert Barron says that C. S. Lewis understood "that Christianity is primarily a story, a narrative. It's the narrative of these great things that God has done. From creation, through the choosing of a people Israel, through the sending of a messiah and the achieving of salvation." C. S. Lewis understood the importance of a good story, and he wrote many of them.

Now, there are lots of great books that contain epic stories, but it is in the pages of the Bible that we read OUR great story. In the Bible, God uses an epic narrative to stir our imaginations and shape our lives. Most importantly, he reveals his Son and the story of his life, death and resurrection. If you claim to be a Christian, this is the story that has changed your life. Maybe you hadn't thought of it that way, but through this story told to you in some fashion, Jesus was revealed to you and everything began to change. Just look at our reading for today. Jesus tells the Scripture narrative from the beginning and reveals himself to the two men as they take communion—breaking the bread together. This is our story!

Every summer I try to pick up a novel and read a great story under a big tree or on a sandy beach. I find that during the summer I have a little more time and a bit less going on. It's funny how that works. For the Church and our calendar Ordinary Time falls during the summer. So if you started this devotional book on the first Sunday of Ordinary Time, it started right around the beginning of summer time. Great timing! If you're reading at another time that's okay, it never hurts to read a good book!

This week, I want to continue the faithful imaginative work that we started last week and keep engaging our great story. Because being shaped by the story of God found in the pages of the Bible should be an ordinary part of every Christian's life.

What is your favorite story? Why do you like it so much? Take some time to reflect on how the story of God has changed your life, then find someone to share that with this week.

Meditation ::.

"I say 'getting back into the story of God' because a dominant error of some Christians is to say, 'I must bring God into my story.' The ancient understanding is that God joins the story of humanity to take us into his story. There is a world of difference. One narcissistic; the other God-oriented. It will change your entire spiritual life when you realize that your life is joined to God's story."

— from *Ancient Future Worship* by Robert Webber

You saw this in yesterday's reading. The entire narrative of Scripture is a story always pointing to Jesus and the creative love and redemption God stirs in our midst and invites us to participate in. The story begins in Genesis 1, with God's love on display as his words come to life. In the middle of this perfect creation that reflects a perfect creator, humanity is formed, the very best and most visible expression of God's image and heart. It's these human beings that God invites into the story, not as passive pawns or animated robots but as active participants in the ongoing story he is writing. Even when the image is shattered to pieces and humanity fails, God keeps inviting humanity to participate, to be restored and bring blessing to all of creation.

In Genesis 12:2 Abraham is told, "I will make you into a great nation, and I will bless you; I will make your name great, and you will be a blessing." Do you ever wonder what your place is in the story? Me too, and that is where it gets exciting. We're invited to participate and to receive our place in God's great story—in what he is up to in this world. We are created in God's image and saved by his crucified Son. Now he invites us to participate in his cross-carrying, life-giving work of being a blessing, of living and sharing the story of love and redemption!

What do you perceive God is up to in your world and surroundings? How can you be a blessing to those you encounter and participate in what he is doing?

Meditation ::.

"When we enter the story of the Gospel of Mark, we enter a world of conflict and suspense, a world of surprising reversals and strange ironies, a world of riddles and hidden meaning, a world of subversive actions and political intrigues. And the protagonist—Jesus—is most surprising of all. The Gospel of Mark deals with great issues—life and death, good and evil, God and Satan, triumph and failure, human morality and human destiny. It is not a simple story in which virtue easily triumphs over vice, nor is it a collection of moral instructions for life. The narrative offers not simple answers but tough challenges ..."

— from *Mark as Story* by David Rhoads, Joanna Dewey
and Donald Michie

Is that not compelling? If those descriptive words were in a movie trailer, I'd be there! Opening night probably.

It resonates deeply in all of us that we need God to come to us, to breathe life into our dry bones and bring growth from the barren soil of our hearts. I think of our reading for today and the three friends who cut a whole through the roof to lower their paralyzed buddy down to Jesus. This story always stirs in me the notion I need to do whatever it takes to get into the presence of Jesus and just as importantly to get my friends into the presence of Jesus.

As we focus on this epic story of God and as we read the Gospel of Mark this week, look for how you fit into this story. Don't simply look for moral truths or dos and don'ts—that's too often our Christian default. Read this grand narrative like you might watch a movie. Let the characters inspire you and shape your heart and mind. See yourself in these pages and then live the story as one Jesus looks to and says, "Come, follow me."

Have you ever felt Jesus asking you to come and follow him? This is a call to participate in his story, in what he is doing in this world. Have you or are you responding to that call?

Meditation ::.

"Story authority, as Jesus knew only too well, is the authority that really works. Throw a rule book at peoples' heads, or offer them a list of doctrines, and they can duck or avoid it, or simply disagree and go away. Tell them a story, though, and you invite them to come into a different world; you invite them to share a worldview or better still a 'God-view.' That, actually, is what the parables are all about. They offer, as all genuine Christian storytelling does, a worldview which, as someone comes into it and finds how compelling it is, quietly shatters the worldview that they were in already. Stories determine how people see themselves and how they see the world. Stories determine how they experience God, and the world, and themselves, and others. Great revolutionary movements have told stories about the past and present and future. They have invited people to see themselves in that light, and people's lives have been changed. If that happens at a merely human level, how much more when it is God himself, the creator, breathing through his word."

— from *How Can the Bible Be Authoritative* by N. T. Wright

Jesus was the world's best storyteller. We his stories parables, and they have shaped worldviews and changed lives. Jesus always tells stories with the purpose of speaking a better world into existence. In fact, his parables are a microcosm of the greater gospel narrative. One of these is the parable of the Prodigal Son in which we see the greater story of God reflected: A rebellious son with a loving father who eagerly waits for his return. A jealous brother who, in doing everything right, is actually doing it all wrong.

The story draws us in, and we can relate to it on multiple levels. We've all been the lost son. We've all been the self-righteous brother. And we all have a loving father who is waiting for us. It's in stories like this that we can begin to understand the life-giving love available to us.

What are we doing with the love and grace that our Heavenly Father continually lavishes upon us?

Today's reading recounts a radical and subversive story Jesus told religious people to shake them out of their comfortable, keep-it-clean, holy existence. In this story, Jesus blurs the lines, calls traditions into question, unsettles the norms. Story has a unique ability to do this. You may have found that it's pretty hard to argue people into changing their minds. But a story, a compelling, unsettling, questions-raising narrative, has the potential to change everything.

That's what it did for me. For a long time as a young, zealous Christian, I wasn't sure what it meant to love my neighbor. Or why would Jesus command me to love my enemy and pray for anybody who would try and do me harm.

When I ran into the parable of the Good Samaritan, Jesus captured my imagination and showed me what it meant to love God and love my neighbor. As I dug into the story, I began to see an example of true holiness and even began to get a glimpse of what it might mean to not only love my neighbor but to even love my enemy.

Here is what Brad Young, author of *The Parables: Jewish Tradition and Christian Interpretation*, says about this parable: "This parable settles a bewildering issue that pertains to love of God and love of humanity. Who is one's neighbor? How far does love extend? How should Leviticus 19:18 be translated? Does it read, 'Love your friends'? Perhaps it should be translated, 'Love even your enemies.'"

Jesus told me a story in this parable. He communicated that in order for me to love God I must love my neighbor and even my enemy. I must look out for anybody whose path I cross that needs help, love or kindness. I began to learn through this story that in loving people around me, I'm loving God. My holiness and Christlikeness is not wrapped up in being clean and pure but in getting down on my knees and serving, even when it might cost me what some consider holiness. I learned that in this parable, a whole new world was created, where love was the rule and holiness was redefined by Jesus and his work on the cross, instead of just being right about "Church stuff."

How might this parable challenge you, your assumptions and your safe, holy life? What are the implications of this for you today?

Have you ever watched a movie and been inspired by a character to do what they do, to live how they live? There are extremes to this, have you ever heard of any of the real life superheroes that occupy some of our cities? There's Mr. Extreme in San Diego, The Dark Guardian and Nyx in New York, Phoenix Jones in Seattle and The Crimson Fist in Atlanta. Yeah, they're the real deal!

One time I was harmlessly sitting on my couch playing on my phone when a figure that resembled a Ninja Turtle jumped from the shadows and pummeled me with a duct-taped blue and sliver sword. A similar thing happen one time but it was Spider-Man who attacked. And now that I think about it this has happened with Batman, Jake the Pirate and various Transformer characters, all who had a striking resemblance to my 5-year-old son Jack. (I guess playing games on your iPhone is a crime when it's play time in our house!)

It's funny and powerful how a good story can stir a person to action. We often see this in kids, don't we? But that storied inspiration shouldn't stop when we grow up. I've been inspired and energized by many movies and books to take action, think differently or just love better. A good story shapes the hearts and imaginations of people, and it's our filled imaginations that then prompt action.

Our call is to be shaped by and then respond to this true story we find in the Scripture. It's an invitation to be on mission with God in our broken world—a God who sounds a lot more powerful in Psalm 121 than any superhero. Let's make sure we let this story move us to action instead of becoming something nice and sentimental.

> How are you participating in God's ongoing story of love and redemption? What cause or organization have you partnered with to live and tell the story?

FAITH

ORDINARY TIME :: SUNDAY #5

2 Samuel 1:1, 17-27 | 2 Corinthians 8:7-15
Psalm 130 | Mark 5:21-43

"Now faith is confidence in what we hope for and assurance about what we do not see" (Hebrews 11:1).

I like how Eugene Peterson puts it in The Message: "The fundamental fact of existence is that this trust in God, this faith, is the firm foundation under everything that makes life worth living. It's our handle on what we can't see."

Faith is all about an understanding deep in our bones that what we can see is not all there is. What we've been told and promised by God is as real, if not more real, than anything we can see, touch or taste.

One extremely important thing to realize is that faith, when truly encountered, may not do away with doubt (we'll talk about that later); but it will, by its very nature, come alive and prompt movement toward obedience, moving us deeper into trust and action for the benefit of our neighbors .

Faith will never simply stay in one's head and heart. Once received, it will always become a verb!

When you look at the people in Hebrews 11, none of them are known simply for their adherence to a set of beliefs. They are known for what they did in response to God, who asked them to take action on promises they often couldn't see.

Is your faith primarily a set of beliefs rattling around in your head? Or is it a verb, an action for you? How are you living it out?

What is the opposite of faith? If I were to poll a group of random people, religious and non-religious, I believe most of us would answer "doubt."

Here is what Anne Lamott writes in her book *Plan B: Further Thoughts on Faith*:

"I have a lot of faith. But I am also afraid a lot, and have no real certainty about anything. I remembered something Father Tom had told me—that the opposite of faith is not doubt, but certainty. Certainty is missing the point entirely. Faith includes noticing the mess, the emptiness and discomfort, and letting it be there until some light returns."

The opposite of faith can't be doubt, questions or fear. The Bible would be sharing the wrong stories if that were the case. All the biblical characters known for their faith, including Abraham, had questions, expressed doubts and experienced fear and failure. If any of those things were the opposite of having faith, we would all be in big trouble. Does this cause you to breathe a huge sigh of relief? It does for me.

If doubt is the opposite of faith and some kind of sickness to be removed, we should probably stop reading the Psalms and get rid of the book of Ecclesiastes. We all experience doubt and questions as a natural part of life. But as those who look beyond what we can see and feel, we are able to take the next step and live daily in light of the resurrection, with the words and life of Jesus before us.

It's when we are certain that we lose our humility and ability to trust God for that next step. Certainty leaves no room for building an ark or hearing news from an angel. Certainty leaves no room for growth because growth inherently includes change. Maybe when Paul talks about testing everything (verse 21), he's talking about having faith rather than certainty. Maybe he is encouraging you and I to be open to the Spirit of God rather than holding tightly to the truth you experienced yesterday. Jesus, the truth, is always drawing you into tomorrow, to faith for a new day.

Where do you need to have more faith and less certainty in your life?

WEDNESDAY // DAY 32
READING :: 1 Corinthians 8:1-13

Yesterday I asked whether the opposite of faith is doubt or certainty. Today we get to the bottom of this question with the help of none other than the Pope. In the meditation that follows, Pope Francis suggests that the opposite of faith isn't doubt, it isn't even certainty, but rather, it is idolatry. Do you hear the game show bells going off? I believe our friend the Pope has nailed it.

The exact opposite of faith in God and the true and beautiful life he has laid out before us is having faith in some other path—some other being or good or god that you believe to be what you really need for abundant life.

Often we idolize ourselves. We think we've figured out the best plan for our lives, the best way forward and the most carefully reasoned story we should be living. For this reason, we often turn ourselves into a god, placing faith only in our limited abilities. Others of us turn money into a god—thinking just enough will save us. Or relationships or influence or safety. Anything we think we've always wanted that we think will fix everything.

It's not doubt. It's not certainty. It's our idolatry of the gifts God has given us that is truly the opposite of our faith.

Meditation ::.

"Faith, tied as it is to conversion, is the opposite of idolatry; it breaks with idols to turn to the living God in a personal encounter. Believing means entrusting oneself to a merciful love which always accepts and pardons, which sustains and directs our lives, and which shows its power by its ability to make straight the crooked lines of our history. Faith consists in the willingness to let ourselves be constantly transformed and renewed by God's call. Herein lies the paradox: by constantly turning towards the Lord, we discover a sure path which liberates us from the dissolution imposed upon us by idols."

— from the *Encyclical Letter Lumen Fidei*
or *The Light of Faith* by Pope Francis

What are your idols? How can you lay them down and
put your faith in God alone?

Do you ever wonder how you're gonna get to tomorrow? The way forward is unclear and life seems so hard and confusing. You can't seem to reason your way forward. You can't buy your way to happiness. You just keep waking up in the same old mess. I have good news: Faith is our way forward!

Galatians 3 tells us we can try to live by the law, our efforts or our own power and ability, but we are assured that the righteous will live by faith. The wise will realize this is really the only way forward. Every other path is bleak, lacking the hope and love that we all long for.

The only way forward is faith.

For people like Noah, faith was an action, not a feeling. Faith was not just a set of beliefs in his head or heart. He did crazy things like building an ark! His actions were—to those only taking into account what they could see or surmise by the signs of the time—crazy! Pretty much the entire list of people in Hebrews 11 follow the same pattern: They took action in counter-intuitive and nonsensical ways. Reason wasn't their way forward. Success and popularity weren't their way forward. Neither were effort and ability. Faith was and is the only way forward for the people of God.

Faith is about living in ways that prove you actually believe in God and have faith that where he leads and how he orders things is the best way. Maybe you have heard of the term "practical atheists." These are people who believe in Jesus and claim to be Christians but with their actions prove the only one they really believe in is themselves—their reason, their understanding, their own efforts. They live like God doesn't matter.

Having faith is about living and acting as God wills and desires. It's about embracing the path laid out before us despite its difficulty, its cross, or the descent it requires. This is the example we've been given in Jesus and live through his Spirit.

> Could anyone mistake you for a practical atheist? What are the obedient actions in your life that show the world your faith?

In high school, my best friend lived about 30 minutes away. His dad was a pastor, his youth group was huge, and he was my best friend! So for good and holy reasons, I would steal my mom's car and drive to visit him.

One particular time I remember talking to myself as I was driving. I was beating myself up about how little I was praying. I wasn't taking time out of my day to get away to a quiet place and be with Jesus. But as if Jesus were in the car with me or something, I began to hear, "What are you doing right now? What do you call this? Could these words and thoughts be an interaction with someone other then yourself?" I began to get this overwhelming sense that Jesus wasn't coming down on me. He was there and hearing my innermost thoughts and my heart's desires, struggles and fears. He was always there, always listening, always present. I just needed to be aware.

We often think we need to get away to a quiet place to connect with God. Yes, that is a good and faith-building practice, but just as important is being aware of God in the car, your living room and in all the moments of your day. Faith can't be relegated to your church or prayer closet; it has to be all the time, all of your moments, all of your days.

Meditation ::.

"Genuine faith is never satisfied with religious ways of doing things— Sabbath worship or an hour or a half-hour of each day. Christianity is nothing else but faith right in the middle of actual life and weekdays. But we have reduced it to quiet hours, thereby indirectly admitting that we are not really being Christians. That we should have quiet times to think about God—this seems so elevated and beautiful, so solemn. It is so hypocritical, because in this way we exempt daily life from authentic worship of God. Anyone who does not take up the task in everyday life and in the living room should just keep quiet, because Sunday vistas into eternity are nothing but air."

— from *Provocations: Spiritual Writings of Kierkegaard*

Do you relegate your faith to a place or time? How can you live your faith in all the places and spaces of your life?

Part of our issue with faith comes from a commonly held notion that you've either got it or you don't. We often think people "come to faith" in an instant and then with faith in their back pockets, they try to follow Jesus. Faith becomes just another possession instead of the gift it actually is.

Did you know that faith, the very thing that bolsters your "yes" to God, is a gift from God? I remember hearing this in a theology class and thinking, "I need God's grace even to say yes to God's grace?" The thought blew my mind but also resonated on a deep, fundamental level. I knew it was true. It's true because in Christ, this is exactly what God has given us. As a gift, faith must be received, and God's normal operating procedure is that it must be received new every morning—just as it is provided freely every morning and in every moment.

This thought that has stuck with me for the last fifteen years is something I picked up from theologian Karl Barth. In today's meditation Barth writes to a man who confesses to lack faith, a man I identify with all too often.

Meditation ::.

"Yes, indeed—who does not lack faith? Who can believe? Certainly no one would believe if he maintained that he 'had' faith, so that nothing was lacking to him, and that he 'could' believe. Whoever believes, knows and confesses that he cannot 'by his own understanding and power' in any way believe … He will say 'I believe' only in and with the entreaty, 'Lord, help my unbelief.' For this very reason he will not suppose that he has his faith, but will hope and hope and hope for it as the Israelites hoped afresh every morning for the manna in the wilderness. And when he receives this faith afresh, he will also daily activate it anew."

— from *Evangelical Theology: An Introduction* by Karl Barth

Do you receive the gift of faith God has for you every morning of every day? How might you activate your faith anew, every morning?

LOVE

ORDINARY TIME :: SUNDAY #6

| 2 Samuel 5:1-5, 9-10 | 2 Corinthians 12:2-10 |
| Psalm 48 | Mark 6:1-13 |

Most of us know in our heads that love isn't an emotion, but I'm not sure we believe it. I mean the belief that is deep down in your bones, the belief that spills out even when you don't mean for it to, the belief that is so deep it guides your actions and words even when you're not aware of it.

Because we most often believe love is an emotion, we say things like, "I love cheeseburgers," or "I love football" or maybe "I love money." We use these words because we have experienced an emotional response when we bit into our first In-N-Out cheeseburger, watched our favorite football team or felt the power or security of having enough money. We've equated these emotions to the idea of love.

We even say that we love people when we experience these heavy emotions.

I remember telling my wife that I loved her for the first time. She was getting ready to move to California; I was going to be living in Nashville. As the distance began to set in, I realized how much I liked her, how sad I was that she was leaving, how bummed I was that we wouldn't get to eat pizza and drink cider on the cardboard box in my apartment. Then there was fear, the fear that with every mile west, a corresponding distance would grow in our hearts. All this emotion led to me blurting out, "I love you." I felt it; I believed it; I said it.

We've been married for seven years now, and I've realized that the real love I now have for my wife didn't begin with those romantic emotions I described. It began on the day I said "I do." It began on the day we were married (or maybe a little before that). True love started with my commitment to always and forever move and act with her in mind. I made a choice to always choose her, not just have feelings for her.

God has moved decisively in your direction in his Son, Jesus. He loves you. Let that truth sink deep into your bones in this week.

When have you confused emotions with love? How does it feel to be loved decisively by God—and how can you love him back with more than your feelings?

Have you ever wondered how you learned to smile? Is it innate, in your DNA? Or do you have to learn to smile from someone who smiles at you?

This is the question we are pondering today as we read the following meditation. The author proposes that we learned to smile because our mothers and fathers smiled on us. Likewise, we learned to love because we have been loved deeply by our fathers and our mothers.

As I think of people who don't smile often and who love poorly—and we all know these people and would even admit to being these people all too often—I'm filled with compassion. Because it is these people who have too seldom been smiled upon and loved too little unconditionally. As you read the following meditation, be filled with gratitude for every little ordinary smile you've been given. Be filled with thankfulness for every ordinary act of love you've been shown. Each one is a gift. Be moved to an open, active love for your neighbor, your friend and even your enemy.

Meditation ::.

"God interprets himself to man as love in the same way: he radiates love, which kindles the light of love in the heart of man, and it is precisely this light that allows man to perceive this, the absolute Love: "For it is God who said, 'Let light shine out of darkness,' who has shown in our hearts to give the light of the knowledge of the glory of God in the face of Christ" (2 Corinthians 4:6). In this face, the primal foundation of being smiles at us as a mother and as a father. Insofar as we are his creatures, the seed of love lies dormant within us as the image of God (*imago*). But just as no child can be awakened to love without being loved, so too no human heart can come to an understanding of God without the free gift of his grace—in the image of his Son."

— from *Love Alone is Credible* by Hans Urs Von Balthasar

You have been smiled on by your Heavenly Father—what a blessing!
Now go smile on a neighbor, stranger or enemy today.

I attended a theology conference at Fuller Seminary in Los Angeles last year. During that conference, N. T. Wright said this:

"Love is not our duty, it is our destiny. Love is the language they speak in the new creation and we get to learn it here. Oh, it's difficult. There are lots of irregular verbs. There is vocabulary that will be very difficult to get into your head and your heart, to get your tongue around. But learn it, and one day you will be singing in it. And faith and hope are pretty much the same. You have to practice them."

I, for one, need more practice loving than I would like to admit. I live compelled to love myself and watch out for my own wants and whims. When I do love, if you can call it that, it's often out of some kind of obligation or duty because I believe in Jesus and call myself a Christian.

Have you ever loved because you were supposed to, because it was your Christian duty or something? We all have, right? I don't think N. T. Wright is telling us this is bad, that if you are loving out of some kind of obligation you're missing the point entirely, but what I do think he's saying is that love is the language of heaven, and you have to learn it and learn it slowly. There will be times when it will feel forced or fake or dutiful to speak this language, but the more you speak it, practice it, just do it, the more it will become your native tongue, instead of foreign words that you fumble over.

Love is our destiny because the Kingdom of God—living where Jesus rules and reigns—is our destiny. You might call it heaven.

We don't do it perfectly now. It might feel forced at times. But the more you learn to live and speak the love that is poured out on us in Christ (verse 14), the more it will become natural, ordinary even.

Have you ever learned a foreign language? Was it hard?
How might you learn the language of love today?

Meditation ::.

"As soon as love dwells on itself, it is out of its element. What does dwelling on itself mean? It means that love itself becomes an object. But an object is always a dangerous matter when one is supposed to move forward; an object is like a finite fixed point, like a boundary and a halting, a dangerous matter of infinitude. That is to say, love itself cannot infinitely become an object ..."

Kierkegaard goes on to explain:

"Think of an arrow flying, as is said, with the speed of an arrow. Imagine that it for an instant has an impulse to want to dwell on itself, perhaps in order to see how far it has come, or how high it is soaring above the earth, or how its speed compares with the speed of another arrow that is also flying with the speed of an arrow—in that same second the arrow falls to the ground."

— from *Works of Love* by Søren Kierkegaard.

We see in this meditation that love has a direction. It is always moving toward an "other." When, if even for a second, we try to act for our own benefit and for the sake of being recognized, we are a resounding gong and a clanging cymbal (1 Corinthians 13:1). The very love that is pulsating through our veins and humming in our heads falls to the ground when we attempt to make it about ourselves, when we turn inward as an object instead of outward as a lover.

How often do you love out of selfish intent, to get recognized or receive credit? What act of secret, selfless love might you do for someone today?

I'm an early adopter. That means I get the new gadget or sign up for the new website when everybody else is still weighing the pros and cons. I've waited in line for the better part of a day for a first generation iPhone and have beta-tested several social media websites. I only know one person who signed up for Twitter before I did. (You can give me a high five later.)

Not only am I an early adopter, but I am also an evangelist—that person who loves what they've got and has to tell everybody about it. Did you know that Apple actually has a job title "Chief Evangelist"? Sign me up; I'm in!

But one thing that comes with being an early adopter and gadget evangelist is that I am also a fickle friend. I have the capacity to jump from one love to the next at the drop of a hat. I love something one minute and the next have forgotten about it.

Love, by its nature, calls for a certain type of exclusivity. For example, you can't really love an iPhone and an Android at the same time. Matthew 6:24 says it all, "No one can serve two masters. Either you will hate the one and love the other, or you will be devoted to the one and despise the other."

Our Scripture reading today is a hard one. People go round and round about what Jesus really meant when he said you must hate your father, mother, wife, children. Beneath the multiple layers of this passage, one thing it definitely gets at is the exclusive nature of love.

I believe the love I have for my wife, my kids and my friends and enemies is somehow enabled by the love I have been given. Only because I have been given it, am I now able to give it. And maybe the exclusive love from a person is a beacon, a sign post of the love God has for us in Jesus, inviting us to participate in it through the Spirit and calling us to share it in community.

What is competing for your exclusive, action-evoking love for God?

Recently people have been discussing whether or not Christians really need to go to church. People I respect and who have been influential in my faith formation have come out and said that church—Sunday, pew-sitting, worship-singing, communion-taking, sermon-listening church—is unnecessary at best and optional at most.

Now, I get where they are coming from. I understand that church isn't a building. I've even said things like, "Jesus didn't call us to go to church; he called us to *be* the church." And can we find community, worship and teaching in our living rooms or at the park with our friends? Sure. But I wonder if love, the kind of love we've been thinking and praying about this week, has any better place to be worked out than in the context of a weekly, gathered body of people like the church.

When I do church in my living room or with my friends, how often am I crossing paths with that guy who annoys me or the lady who I disagree with or that guy who pulls his pants up to his chest? Part of the beauty of church, the kind we attend weekly in order to learn, pray and participate, is that we are invited to interact with people we would never sit by or talk to otherwise.

At my church, we are given the opportunity every week to do what we call "passing the peace." The goal of this practice is to be at peace, to be reconciled, with the very people with whom you will soon approach the Lord's table. You're going to be receiving the body and blood of Jesus together; you've both received grace upon grace in ways you could never deserve. So it's important to remember you must extend that grace as well—to people who aren't like you, to people you don't like, even to people who have done you wrong. Because let's be honest: There are all types in the churches we go to.

We must learn the way of love. And I believe a worshiping church community is the perfect context to be reminded of the love you've been shown and to have the opportunity to work out the love you're called to show.

How is your church helping you to experience and share God's love?

VIRTUE

2 Samuel 6:1-5, 12-19 | Ephesians 1:3-14
Psalm 24 | Mark 6:14-29

Most likely, if you're a follower of Jesus, you've asked him, "What must I do, Jesus?" I think we all want to please God on some level, to live the right way. That's what this week is all about.

The best known of the virtues are faith, hope and love. The Apostle Paul groups these together in many places throughout Scripture. These words have a relationship; they share a particular kind of energy or movement. Many respected thinkers in the Christian tradition have said that virtues answer the question, "What must I do?" Here's what N. T. Wright says in his book *After You Believe*:

"My contention … is that the New Testament invites its readers to learn how to be human in this particular way, which will both inform our moral judgments and form our characters so that we can live by their guidance. The name for this way of being human, this kind of transformation of our character, is virtue."

We're all human right? It's the most ordinary thing you can say about a person. But we are all different kinds of humans. The human who wants to live in the way of Jesus will be called to develop certain virtues—primarily those of faith, hope and love. We're not just called to have faith, hope and love. We're not called to think they're important. We are called put faith, hope and love to action in our lives. This is the real definition of virtue.

This week we will focus on how it's possible to embrace these virtues in our everyday life in order to please God, and how faith, hope and love work together for this aim.

> When is the last time you asked Jesus, "What must I do?"
> What is he calling you to do? What part of your character
> does he want to grow this week?

A habit is something you've done so much that you don't even think about it anymore—you just do it. It's really hard to break a habit.

A friend of mine is a musician and he had a horrible habit of chewing his fingernails. He would chew his nails so much that his fingers would bleed. And when you play the guitar in front of hundreds of people on a regular basis, it becomes a pretty visible habit. Someone finally gave him a tip so he could break this habit: nail polish. Specifically, some clear nail polish that tasted like that stuff you don't want to step in at the dog park. So my friend lathered it on. He quickly broke his nail-biting habit and impressed all the ladies with this beautiful, shiny nails. Win, win!

We all probably have a bad habit we would like to stop. But what about starting a new habit?

I've tried to start a habit before: running, working out, reading my Bible every morning, praying every meal. It's hard to break a habit, but I think it's even harder to start a habit.

Did you know that some people refer to virtue as a holy habit? My challenge to you would be to start one of these holy habits. There are plenty to choose from. We've talked about the three primary virtues: faith, hope and love. There are also what people call the four cardinal virtues: prudence (wise decision-making), temperance (moderation and self-control) justice and courage. Some people consider countless other things virtues as well.

Do you need to make wiser, more thought-out choices in your life? Maybe you need to form the habit of prudence. Do you need to quit playing it safe and shying away from sharing your faith with a friend or taking that opportunity at your school or job? Maybe you need to learn how to develop the holy habit of being courageous.

> What holy habit can you start today? Whatever it might be, look through the list or think of your own, and begin to take steps to forming it in your life today.

WENESDAY // DAY 46
READING :: Titus 2:1-15

Meditation ::.

"Virtue, to put it bluntly, is a revolutionary idea in today's world—and today's church. But the revolution is one we badly need ... After you believe, you need to develop Christian character by practicing the specifically Christian 'virtues.' To make wise moral decisions, you need not just to 'know the rules' or 'discover who you really are,' but to develop Christian virtue. And to give wise leadership in our wider society in the confusing and dangerous time we live in, we urgently need people whose characters have been formed in much the same way. We've had enough of pragmatists and self-seeking risk-takers. We need people of character ... The key to it all, though, is that the Christian vision of virtue, of character that has become second nature, is precisely all about discovering what it means to be truly human—human in a way most of us never imagine."

— from *After You Believe* by N. T. Wright

Virtue as revolution? This quote just may change how you think about virtue. It is not about earning your salvation or just being a good person. It's about learning how to live once you've believed in God and put your citizenship in heaven. Virtue is living by the family values of our Father, who dwells and reigns in heaven. Virtue is about creating the habits of heaven that we have learned from our Father, see modeled by Jesus and are continually inspired to live by the Spirit.

Here's a counter-intuitive fact: That which seems revolutionary and extraordinary in the space and time we currently occupy is the most ordinary thing in the Kingdom of God—that space and place we claim as our residence as people who follow King Jesus. When we live out faith, hope and love according to the example we see in Jesus it will look extraordinary. But faith, hope and love were the most ordinary of things for Jesus and as we follow him, they will become ordinary for us as well.

Are the virtues of Jesus an ordinary part of your life? What are you doing to become a more ordinary Jesus-follower?

In our Scripture reading for today, we find the answer to our opening question of the week: "What must I do?" The answer lies in Jesus' famous words, "I am the way, the truth and the life."

It's here that we learn how Jesus works. He doesn't give abstract directions or some nebulous truth. He doesn't give you eternal life and then tell you, "Good luck." No, in all things Jesus gives us himself. We find that he is the way, he is the truth and he is the life we always wanted. All our deepest longings are wrapped up in the person of Jesus, the one who is constantly giving himself to us.

"What must I do?" In Mark 10, the rich man finds out that the answer is, "Follow me."

Let's keep this in mind as we step into a conversation about virtue. If you want faith, Jesus is going to give you himself. If you want hope, again, Jesus is going to give you himself. And if you want love, you guessed it you're gonna get Jesus! I could go on, but I think you get the point.

Jesus gives us himself and in him we are able to begin to live a life of virtue. He enables us to take action and make things like faith, hope and love ordinary habits of our everyday life. That's because Jesus was the ultimate example of virtue, of what a life firmly rooted in the rule and reign of our Father looks like. Everything Jesus believed to be true he lived without fear or caution. There was no division in his life between theory and practice, between belief and action.

We'll talk more about following Jesus and living by his example, but today may we realize that the goal of all our wise and righteous choices, our virtuous living, is to imitate Jesus. Because it is Jesus who perfectly embodies everything we believe to be a virtue. And our only hope is him!

What is the most impressive virtue you see in the life of Jesus?
How might you begin to follow Jesus into this way of life?

Meditation ::.

"This is an age for spiritual heroes—a time for men and women to be heroic in faith and in spiritual character and power. The greatest danger to the Christian church today is that of pitching its message too low. Holiness and devotion must now come forth from the closet and the chapel to possess the street and the factory, the schoolroom and the boardroom, the scientific laboratory and the governmental office. Instead of a select few making religion their life, with the power and inspiration realized through the spiritual disciplines, all of us can make our daily lives and vocations be 'the house God and the gate of heaven.' It can—and must—happen. And it will happen. The living Christ will make it happen through us as we dwell with him in life appropriately disciplined in the spiritual Kingdom of God. The Spirit of the Disciplines is nothing but the love of Jesus, with resolute will to be like him whom we love."

— from *The Spirit of the Disciplines* by Dallas Willard

An important way to cultivate virtue is through the practice of spiritual disciplines. Spiritual disciplines are things like prayer, Bible-reading, fasting, solitude, service and worship, among others. These things are called "disciplines" because one has to strive with all the energy of Christ that's in us to live in the way of Christ, to say yes to him, to be holy. Disciplines don't produce virtue in and of themselves, but they create much-needed space for Christ's power to be at work in us.

Trying to be more virtuous on our own will lead to frustration, mediocrity and futility. Our only hope for true Kingdom virtue, true and authentic holiness is the presence and power of God, Father, Son and Holy Spirit. Don't attempt it on your own. Don't settle for anything less. Virtuous living isn't an easy task, but luckily it's a task we are equipped to do by the One who asks us to do it. And this is the only way to succeed.

Do you ever settle for mediocre? Do you live a life that is less than holy? Pray to receive the power of Christ so that you might live in holiness and devotion to King Jesus.

Virtue, holy habits and living like Jesus are pretty intimidating ideas. When people say things like "you should be like Jesus" or "you need to be holy," our natural response is, "Say what?" Maybe, as you thought through the Scriptures and devotions for this week, you had a similar response. I think today's Scripture might help us put it all together and find some hope for this kind of life.

Focus on Matthew 25:23: "You have been faithful with a few things; I will put you in charge of many things. Come and share your master's happiness!"

With anything you do, any skill you develop or holy habit you form, the first step is always a small step. God knows our hearts and limitations. He's not looking for spiritual giants who have it all together and already live perfect lives. God is just looking for a start—for a little nugget of faith to be put into practice today so that he can give it back to you, two-fold, tomorrow.

Have you ever been asked to play in a professional football game? Did you suit up and jump into the starting lineup no problem? Even if you are a professional football player and reading this book you didn't just jump onto the field the first time you ever picked up a football or put on the pads. It took years of practice and discipline and even failure to finally get to play in a real game. You had to be faithful in learning the little things, in doing the basics a million times before you ever got the chance to do the big things.

Here is the cool thing: We will be ready to do the big things because we have done the little things a million times. We develop the skill and virtue while being faithful in the everyday moments of life.

So be faithful in the little things. Take one step. Read one verse. Be brave one time. Then you'll be ready to be faithful, focused, wise and brave in all the big things that come your way.

> How might you take one small step toward a life of virtue?
> What is one little thing could you begin to do today?

FEAR

ORDINARY TIME :: SUNDAY #8

2 Samuel 7:1-14	Ephesians 2:11-22
Psalm 89:20-37	Mark 6:30-34, 53-56

To fear or not to fear, that is the question. If you read through your Bible or just do an internet search for "fear in the Bible," you'll get a lot of verses. Some say "fear not," and a dozen others say you need a little fear and trembling. So which is it?

"Moses said to the people, 'Do not be afraid. God has come to test you, so that the fear of God will be with you to keep you from sinning' " (Exodus 20:20).

Is it as simple as what or who you fear? Psalm 27 asks the question, "Whom shall I fear?" And I think it's good to ask who we should fear, making Psalm 27 our prayer. The fear we are invited to expel in the "fear not" verses is different than the fear we're encouraged to embrace in the "fear God" verses. It's in Scripture that God defines who and how we need engage with fear.

Since the wrong kind of fear is such an ordinary part of our lives in a way that the right kind of fear seldom is, we'll spend this week pondering how to engage fear for our good!

Meditation ::.

" 'Fear of God' is not cowering, frightened intimidation. Those who fear God are not wimps and are not preoccupied with excessive need to please God. They are rather those who have arrived at a *fundamental vision of reality about life with God*, who have enormous power, freedom, and energy to live out that vision. 'Fear of God' is liberating and not restrictive, because it gives confidence about the true shape of the world.

— from *Remember You Are Dust* by Walter Brueggemann

Let that thought stir your heart and imagination toward a new embrace of fear. One that will lead toward freedom and straight into life with God.

Let's start this week by asking what fear God wants to expose and eliminate from our lives, and what kind of fear he wants to cultivate instead.

What does "fear" mean to you? Is it being caught doing something you aren't supposed to be doing? Is it the jitters in your stomach on the first day of school? Or is it when you get in line for the Giant Drop at an amusement park or when you went on your first date? Maybe it's that feeling when you watch a scary movie or when your friend jumped out from behind the bushes. Remember when you were little and you were "afraid of the dark"?

We've all experienced fear that makes us want to run, hide or play dead. The fear that makes us want to avoid what might happen—the terrible "unknown." The fear of being exposed when everything is in the light. But as we talked about yesterday, this isn't the only kind of fear. There is also the fear of the Lord. And this is radically different.

This fear is less about being squashed or punished by an all-powerful God and more about producing reverence and obedience and action. It's the kind of fear you feel when you love someone so much that you fear disappointing them—not because they will punish you, but because they might experience sadness or grief over your actions or inaction. This fear sometimes makes us want to hide and avoid relationship, but ultimately it should make us want to move and act for the good of the one we love.

God is love, and love redefines fear. For the Christian, fear now has to do with our motivation to love and serve God. Fear is when we throw our hands up in the air and proclaim, "I love you so much that I will do whatever it takes to never disappoint you or hurt you."

Of course, meeting God face to face would also induce sheer terror, the "fall down as though I'm dead" kind of fear. It's pretty clear that when people encounter God in the Bible, this is their immediate response; and it would be ours. But without delay, God says, "Do not be afraid" (Revelation 1:17). He is always wanting to redefine fear according to his great love for us.

Do you ever fear disappointing or hurting the people you love most?
What does that fear motivate you to do?
Do you have this kind of fear for God?

68

MEDITATION ::.

"What is true of nature and human nature is also true of the Divine. It is time to reappropriate the importance of holy fear before the God who is the source of the process of creation.

But doesn't 'perfect love cast out fear'? The fear that St. John says is cast out by God's love 'has to do with punishment' (1 John 4:18). Unless we can shed our fear of a vindictive God lurking to strike out through calamity or adversity, we may not be able to stand in holy fear before the One from whom all the mighty powers of creation flow. Absorbing the reality that nothing can separate us from the compassionate love manifested in Christ (Romans 8:39), we can face the blessings and dangers of creation with full consciousness, ready to tread with fear but fundamentally unafraid.

We can face fully that as gifted and as powerful as we may be, we are still small, fragile creatures who walk in the midst of titanic powers that rightly invoke breathtaking awe. It is not that the power of the storm, the intensity of the sunlight, or the passionate nature of love are out to harm us; it is that they are powerful in their working and we must tread carefully in their presence. Only as we learn how to comport ourselves respectfully can we drink deeply of their goodness.

Surely the same is true of the God who sources it all. The Love that knocks at the door of our heart is also the One who spins this world into its teeming, boisterous life."

— from *Weavings* (March/April 1999), "Holy Fear and the Wildness of God," by Robert Corin Morris as found in *A Guide to Prayer for All Who Walk with God*

I love this meditation because it explains that the God who creates everything is on our side. The power that spoke creation into existence is for us. He loves us! This should begin to change and redefine the way we see fear. If nothing can separate us from God's love, what do we have to fear?

How does knowing God is on your side change what you are afraid of?

THURSDAY // DAY 54
READING :: Genesis 22:1-14

The story of Abraham and Isaac in our Scripture today is a familiar one. At first glance, it is not a story about fear, but as we approach the end, we learn that this is exactly what the story is about.

God asks Abraham to sacrifice his son—his son whom he loved. When we read "whom you love" at the end of verse 2, this isn't a trivial throwaway line. We may think, "Of course he loved his son," but we should understand that this son entailed all that Abraham ever wanted and hoped for. This son was the fulfillment of God's promise to Abraham. This son was the culmination of many years of waiting, suffering and wondering if life was even worth living. In this son, Abraham found love. The kind of love that you would give your own life for and would do everything and anything to protect.

It is this son, this son who Abraham loves, about whom God says, "Offer him as a burnt offering." This is biblical speak for "sacrifice him." And that means: "Kill him because God wants you to." What? This seems to make no earthly sense. But the piece of the story that has always fascinated me most are the angel's words as Abraham is about to plunge the knife into his son's chest: "Now I know that you fear God." That's what this whole story is about. The test mentioned at the beginning was all about this fear.

Abraham is seized by the fear of God, loving him more than anything else in the universe, even his beloved son. How scandalous is that! Abraham, above all other relationships, will be faithful and obedient in his relationship with God. Abraham shows us that the fear our Lord desires is obedient fear, the kind of fear that says yes in the face of all else because no other relationship is more important than the one we have with our Heavenly Father.

Today it is our privilege, with the gift of the Scriptures and perspective of Jesus in mind, to know that what was asked of Abraham was freely given by God. In both cases, a son was the sacrifice and love was put on display. Ponder the idea that God feared being separated from you so much that he gave his own life in love on a cross.

Have you ever been obedient to God when it seemed crazy? Why?

"Therefore, my beloved, as you have always obeyed, so now, not only as in my presence but much more in my absence, work out your own salvation with fear and trembling, for it is God who works in you, both to will and to work for his good pleasure" (Philippians 2:12-13).

One of my favorite authors, Søren Kierkegaard wrote a book titled *Fear and Trembling*, in which he thinks about the story of Abraham and Isaac from a very unique angle. He engages this story from the perspective of a person who is ethical above all else; right and wrong are the only things that matter. And from this perspective, the story of God asking Abraham to sacrifice his son just does not compute.

But from the perspective of a person who loves God and has already surrendered his family, friends and possessions to the faith and love that animate his every move—to that person this story makes perfect sense. It doesn't make it easier, but it makes it understandable.

Paul encourages people who love Jesus to work out their salvation with fear and trembling. This makes some Christians nervous because we believe that salvation is by grace alone, though faith alone. But Paul calls for a response to that love and grace. He calls for an arms-thrown-up-in-surrender kind of relationship with God. This type of everyday obedience or fear is hard work. Paul does not say, "Earn your salvation"; he says, "Work out your salvation." Do the hard work of saying yes to Jesus every day, in every moment. Do the hard work of doing the right, true and good thing in the face of opposition and earthly reason.

Let God's love seize you so thoroughly that you, with fear and trembling, say yes each moment of every day—making it the most ordinary thing you do.

Is saying yes to Jesus ordinary for you? How are you working out the free gift of salvation with fear and trembling, moment by moment?

Meditation ::.

"If we believe in Christ, fear does not isolate us from God. On the contrary, it leads us deeper in community with him. Christian faith in God is essentially fellowship with Christ, and fellowship with Christ is essentially fellowship with the Christ who was tempted and assailed, who suffered and was forsaken. In our anxiety we participate in Christ's anxiety; for in his suffering Christ went through the very fears and anxieties which men and women encounter today."

— from *Jesus Christ For Today's World* by Jürgen Moltmann

What a powerful idea! We can let all the things we fear push us toward Jesus, who has willingly taken them on. He meets us in those fears, takes them on himself and says, "Don't be afraid. I've got this. I'm here."

We can talk about all these lofty ideas of fear—how we shouldn't fear what we don't know or how we should fear God in particular ways. But let's be honest. I fear a lot of things in my everyday life. I fear failure. I fear anonymity. I fear being thought of as stupid and worthless. I fear being thought of as proud and arrogant. I fear my kids getting hurt, my money being taken, my life falling apart. A verse telling me not to fear or a pastor saying, "Don't be afraid," isn't really going to change that. Why shouldn't I fear?

The answer is Jesus.

He not only understands, he meets us in our most vulnerable places, takes on that bone-chilling fear and nails it to the cross.

What are the fears you just can't shake? Could you let those fears push you toward Jesus?

EXAMEN

ORDINARY TIME :: SUNDAY #9

| 2 Samuel 11:1-15 | Ephesians 3:14-21 |
| Psalm 14 | John 6:1-21 |

When is the last time you went in for a medical examination? Why did you go? Let me guess—someone made you. We don't often voluntarily go in for an exam. I mean, who really wants someone poking and prodding at you, looking at you through weird instruments and making sounds of discovery that prompt the thought, "Am I dying?"

All kidding aside, we get exams to be sure we're healthy, find out what's going on in our bodies, measure our status compared to a goal we have set, or make a new goal based on the findings. Sometimes an exam just helps us to stay in touch with ourselves and our doctor so we know what healthy looks like and when something's wrong.

The same is true in our lives with God. We must consistently examine our hearts and minds, remaining open and even ask, "Search me, God, know my heart; test me and know my anxious thoughts" (Psalm 139:23). Essentially, we need to know if we are healthy and connected to God. Where are the parts of our lives that are dark and need attention? Where are we broken and in need of healing through God's love? Where are our temptations, failures and sins?

Unfortunately many Christians never examine their inner lives or let God do it either. So we simply react to symptoms of sin in our lives instead of being proactive, asking God to show us where we need to receive grace and to grow.

During Ordinary Time, we experience the Feast of St. Ignatius of Loyola, the founder of the Society of Jesus. One of his great contributions is what he called the "examination of conscience." Jesuits often refer to it as The Examen because it is its original Spanish name. The idea is that taking personal inventory—examining our inner lives and our relationships with Jesus—should be an ordinary habit. This week we will focus on the Examen, taking time to look inward and ask ourselves: "If my goal is to reflect Jesus, to live in his Kingdom, and if I really want to see him at work in my everyday, ordinary life, how can I make this kind of examination part of my life?"

Are you willing to truly look at your inner life, your heart and mind, before God? Will you open the deepest parts of yourself to God and let the Spirit love you and lead you? If you are, let's Examen.

One of the greatest tools I've encountered for my ordinary life is St. Ignatius' Prayer of Examen. I don't always pray it properly at the end of my day. Sometimes I just incorporate bits of it throughout my day. But it's an awesome practice, however you might engage with it. Here is a version I created, pulling from a handful of places.

THE PRAYER OF EXAMEN

BEGIN :: Become aware of God's love and presence. Remind yourself that God is with you. There is nothing to fear; you are safe and loved.

THANK :: Bring to mind the good things that God has brought into your life, and let gratitude begin to bubble up. What gifts, big or small, has God given you today? Thank him for every good and perfect gift.

REVIEW :: Ask God to show you where you have failed, fallen or sinned in the past day. We're talking about sins both known and unknown. Ask God to bring to mind any and every time you turned from his leading.

NOTICE :: Look back on your day again, each and every thing you did. Relive what you thought about, wanted and felt and desired during those moments. Begin to sense God's activity. When were you cooperating most fully with God, and when were you not?

FORGIVE :: With confidence ask God, the one whose loving presence has been with you and is always with you, to forgive you for all the moments you went your own way. Remember the Lord's Prayer: "Forgive us our debts, as we also have forgiven our debtors" (Matthew 6:12).

RESPOND :: Ask yourself, "Going forward, how can I receive and participate in God's grace, resolving to live as a cooperative partner with God for his glory and the good of my neighbor?

END :: Saint Ignatius recommends you end with The Lord's Prayer, found in Matthew 6:9-13.

Sometimes a good example is the best encouragement. Today, let's learn a little more about the life of St. Ignatius of Loyola. Ignatius was an ordinary guy who encountered Christ's love and was challenged to follow Jesus by the lives of other godly men.

Jesuit priest James Martin shares the following in his book *A Jesuit Guide to (Almost) Everything:* "Ignatius of Loyola is one of the most influential religious founders in Christian history. The religious order that he founded continues to have worldwide influence and is especially known for its work in education and spiritual formation."

But before he was St. Ignatius, he was Íñigo López de Loyola. Martin continues speaking of Ignatius in his younger years, "He was a man given over to the vanities of the world; with a great and vain desire to win fame he delighted especially in the exercise of arms." Martin also says, "Ignatius may be the only saint with a notarized police record: for nighttime brawling with an intent to inflict harm."

From what I can tell, Ignatius was a determined, entrepreneurial type. His early life was marked by ambition, and he was known for his intense temper and his fondness for women. One of thirteen kids in a wealthy family, Ignatius was injured in battle after taking a heroic but ill-advised military stand. While healing, he began to read about the saints of the church, St. Francis and St. Dominic in particular. He thought, I want to be like them; I can do what they do. He wanted to live for Christ with every part of himself.

Martin writes, "Did Ignatius trade ambition in the military life for ambition in the spiritual life? David, my spiritual director in the Jesuit novitiate, put it differently: God used even Ignatius's overweening pride for the good. For no part of a life cannot be transformed by God's love. Even the aspects of ourselves that we consider worthless, or sinful, can be made worthwhile and holy. As the proverb has it, God writes straight with crooked lines."

What part of Ignatius' story inspires you? How might you follow his example and turn your ambitions and desires toward your pursuit of Jesus?

The first time I attended a silent retreat at a Jesuit retreat center, I was really excited. I couldn't wait to pray, read and think about everything that was happening in my life. My wife and I were in the throes of making some pretty huge life decisions, and I was confident God was going to speak to me through my time of silence and prayer, as well as through the retreat speaker for the weekend. He was a well-known Jesuit priest and retreat guide, and I was going to get to sit under his teaching all weekend. Bring it!

As the first session began, I sat in the pew, journal ready for note-taking, ears and heart ready for listening and life ready to be rocked! In the first session, a 25- to 30-minute talk, the only thing the speaker said was, "Jesus loves you and you were created for him." He said it fifteen different ways and told ten different stories to reiterate his point. It was literally the only thing he said.

I walked away thinking: *That's it? Where is the depth, the meat, the life-changing word from on high I was so ready for?* The retreat guide spoke several more times throughout the weekend and always came back to the same point: Jesus loves you and you were created for him.

I was tempted to be disappointed, but as the weekend progressed, I began to realize why St. Ignatius called this his principal and foundation. There is nothing more important than knowing this fundamental truth. We will never move forward in faith, hope and love without this elemental piece: Jesus loves you and you were created for him.

The goal of examining ourselves and practicing the spirituality of St. Ignatius is, strangely enough, not to better know ourselves. The goal is to more rightly see and know God, how he loves us and who he has created us to be.

St. Ignatius begins and ends with this principal and foundation. We can't get past it or move forward without it.

> Do you believe, deep down, that you are loved by God and that nothing is more important? Take some time to ponder this simple but profound truth today.

Meditation ::.

"Self-examination is a practice that facilitates spiritual awakening—an awakening to the presence of God as God really is and an awakening to ourselves as we really are. When practiced rightly, it leads us into a greater sense of God's constant loving presence in our life, it fosters a celebration of our created self, it offers us a safe place to see and name those places where we are not like Christ, and it opens us up to deeper levels of spiritual transformation. Self-examination is the Christian practice that open us to the love we seek."

— from *Sacred Rhythms* by Ruth Haley Barton

The meditation above reinforces our need for self-examination. When we go inward, we are aware of God and become aware of the places where we need him. When we dive into our inner lives with God, Father, Son and Holy Spirit, God begins to press in and renovate our deepest, darkest parts. From this place of knowing how deeply and unconditionally we are loved, we are then able to go and love our neighbor and even do the trickier work Jesus asks of us: "Love your enemies and pray for those who persecute you" (Matthew 5:44).

Henri Nouwen, in his book *The Spirituality of Living*, outlines this pattern beautifully and simply. He says the circle of life and ministry begins in solitude, prayer and examination. It then moves to community, which he defines as "solitude greeting solitude." Finally, the love of God that we experience in prayer and solitude, that we share in community, we give away in service to world. This is ministry.

I think Nouwen is right on. We must begin in prayer and examination, and only then can we faithfully and honestly love our neighbor, our enemy and even our persecutors. God is pleased with our inward journey and then leads us on an outward adventure!

Have you ever experienced God prompting you to take action, to show love to someone during a time of prayer and solitude? Ask God to do that today.

This week, the life and teachings of St. Ignatius of Loyola encouraged us to examine our lives before God and know that he, Love, meets us there. We learned that examination should be an ongoing, ordinary part of a life that seeks after God and is awake to his presence and leading. I want to leave you with one of the practical ways that Ignatian spirituality can help us live lives at the center of God's will.

Have you ever wondered about God's will for your life? Yeah, me too. While trying to make some difficult decisions about my future this year, I read Fr. Timothy Gallagher's book *Discerning the Will of God: An Ignatian Guide to Christian Decision Making*.

To discern the will of God in a specific area, Ignatius has some great insight and exercises. Here are eight steps I gleans from Ignatius in the area of discernment.

1. **Ask the right questions.** "What does God want me to do?"
2. **Embrace the foundation.** Know God's love and be willing to respond.
3. **Desire to live like Jesus** who always did the will of the one who sent him.
4. **Prepare to say yes.** A heart disposed to discernment is a heart ready to say yes to God.
5. **Prioritize worship.** Place going to church and the Eucharist at the center of your discernment.
6. **Submerse yourself in the Gospels** to have the life and ministry of Jesus before you.
7. **Find regular and frequent times to be silent before God.**
8. **Seek out spiritual companionship and direction.** Don't discern alone; do it with pastors and friends.

What tools do you have that help you follow Jesus better? Could you use The Examen or the above steps for discerning God's will in your everyday life?

Head over to the Web Guide to find three more modes of discernment, as well as one of Ignatius' spiritual exercises, Discernment of Spirits.

REAL

2 Samuel 11:26-12:13 | Ephesians 4:1-16
Psalm 51:1-12 | John 6:24-35

Have you ever seen "behind the curtain"? I'm not sure where this phrase comes from, but it makes me think of *The Wizard of Oz*. Dorothy finally arrives at the Emerald City and wants the great and powerful Oz to help her get home. Her trusty canine companion Toto winds up sniffing out the wizard who's just a normal guy behind a curtain. Once Dorothy sees behind the curtain, once she gets a glimpse of the real wizard, she cannot "unsee" the reality, no matter how disappointing it is.

This week, we see "behind the curtain" in the story of Christ and his transfiguration. Many Christians around the world celebrate the Feast of the Transfiguration on August 6, making it an integral part of Ordinary Time. We are focusing on this story because it has the potential to reveal to us what is real in our ordinary lives, as well as what sustains us on this long journey we find ourselves on.

Often, like Dorothy, when we see behind the curtain, we are disappointed. But the reality that the Transfiguration narrative reveals to us is anything but disappointing. The disciples audibly hear God speak—he is real! The reality of the Kingdom of God, this realm where God rules and reigns, is clearly seen! This experience, as frightening as it may have been, causes the disciples to want to set up camp and stay on the mountaintop. The light, beauty and glory are what we all long for. The Kingdom that Jesus says has "come near" in Mark 1:15 is real and present, even if it is typically just out of sight, hidden behind a thin veil.

In all those times of doubt and despair. When the reality of hurt and brokenness that is right in front of our face is all that seems to be real. When it doesn't feel like anything will ever change and hope is possible. It's in these times—and we all know about these times—that the story of the Transfiguration reminds us that there is a reality just beyond what we can see. God is real, he speaks and his Son leads us to participate in the Kingdom of Heaven not just the kingdoms in front of our faces.

Have you ever questioned if God or his Kingdom were real?
What would change if you knew, beyond a shadow of a doubt, that
they were indeed real?

Have you ever been to a retreat or camp and had such an amazing experience that you just wanted to stay in that place, with those friends, in the presence of God forever? I went to a camp like this when I was younger. I had amazing spiritual experiences there, and afterward I wondered why life between camps was boring and ordinary. Why wasn't it like it was at camp? I would catch glimpses of God in my daily life, but it never seemed like he was as present to me as he was on the "mountaintop" of camp.

The Transfiguration is the story of some normal guys following Jesus onto a mountaintop where they're ushered into the presence of God. The curtain or veil is pulled back, and they see what is always there but just out of sight—God and his Kingdom, his overpowering light, goodness and love. They see and experience it.

There's an icon of the Transfiguration that I love. At first glance, you are drawn to Jesus, radiating light and love and everybody bowing down before him. But if you glance to the left, you see Jesus leading the disciples up the mountain. And then to the right, you see Jesus leading the disciples down the mountain. This icon points to a great reality: *You can't stay on the mountain.* Jesus may lead you there and give you a glimpse, but then you have to follow him back down to the ordinary, everyday time and space of life.

Many Bible scholars believe Jesus invited Peter, James and John onto the mountain because he knew what lay before them. He knew the difficulty that would follow. Despite all they would see on the cross and the despair they would experience in his absence, Jesus wanted them to know that even then, in the face of a bloody reality, something even more real was at play. Just behind the curtain there was a good God, not a wizard, who was going to make all things new. Even when the reality in front of your face is dark and ugly, rest assured there's something more real just behind what you can see. This truth can guide and ground you in all the difficult and the ordinary days of your life.

Have you ever had a mountaintop experience with God? How does that encounter with God help you in your everyday life when things are difficult or even just uneventful?

Meditation ::.

"[The Transfiguration] stands as a gateway to the saving events of the gospel, and is as a mirror in which the Christian mystery is seen in its unity. Here we receive that the living and the dead are one in Christ, that the old covenant and the new are inseparable, that the Cross and the glory are of one, that the age to come is already here, that our human nature has a destiny of glory, that in Christ the final word is uttered and in him alone the Father is well pleased. Here the diverse elements in the theology of the New Testament meet."

— from *The Glory of God and the Transfiguration of Christ*
by Arthur Michael Ramsey

The story of the Transfiguration is almost exactly in the middle of each of the three synoptic Gospels: Matthew, Mark and Luke. But our meditation points to something much bigger then its placement by these authors.

The Transfiguration is a gateway because it gives us a glimpse into Jesus' connection to the old covenant, the Law that Moses represents, as well as the Prophets who spoke of God's desires and plans, represented by Elijah. Jesus is the fullness of both the Law and the Prophets. His life, death and resurrection are the beginning of God making all things new. In Christ, the Kingdom has come. In Christ, salvation is available.

Because we can see the whole story from Genesis to Revelation, it may not seem like such a big deal that Jesus and his life were foreshadowed by the Law and the Prophets. But how amazing is it to see a microcosm of God's message and plan in one event, the Transfiguration? Like the disciples, we hear God say, "This is my Son, whom I love." And let's not forget the words that follow: "Listen to him."

What better story to encourage and enliven us to listen and follow Jesus, the Son full of grace, truth and glory?

How might you hear the Father's words—"listen to him"—anew today?

Eugene Peterson translates Romans 12:1-2 this way in *The Message*:

"So here's what I want you to do, God helping you: Take your everyday, ordinary life—your sleeping, eating, going-to-work, and walking-around life—and place it before God as an offering. Embracing what God does for you is the best thing you can do for him. Don't become so well-adjusted to your culture that you fit into it without even thinking. Instead, fix your attention on God. You'll be changed from the inside out. Readily recognize what he wants from you, and quickly respond to it. Unlike the culture around you, always dragging you down to its level of immaturity, God brings the best out of you, develops well-formed maturity in you."

Did you catch that line, "You'll be changed from the inside out"? The word for this in the NIV Bible is *transformation*. That's the goal of offering ourselves, all that we are, to God to be transformed, as 2 Corinthians says, "into his image with ever-increasing glory."

Transformation in Greek here is actually the same word used to describe what happens to Jesus on the mount of Transfiguration. It's typically translated "transfigure" and rightly so. In that moment, we see Jesus and his fullness. He is transfigured, revealed for all that he truly is. But in our passage from Romans, Paul is encouraging you and me to be transformed or transfigured with Christ and into his image. How is that even possible? It's not about getting rid of a few bad habits but it's about a complete change so that we can become like Christ. Andreas Andreopoulos, in his book *This is My Beloved Son*, writes, "The Transfiguration reveals and outlines the whole mystery of salvation. And his transfiguration invites us to transfigure with him."

When we are transfigured or transformed we are becoming more like Christ. That means becoming the fullness of the humanity that God always planned for us to be. We are invited to behold his glory and follow him everyday as a way of becoming like him. This is our participation in his transfiguration.

How have you changed in the past year? Think about Jesus. How might you be transformed to be more like him in the next year?

Meditation ::.

"Don't you often hope: 'Maybe this book, idea, course, trip, job, country or relationship will fulfill my deepest desire.' But as long as you are waiting for that mysterious moment you will go on running helter-skelter, always anxious and restless, always lustful and angry, never fully satisfied. You know that this is the compulsiveness that keeps us going and busy, but at the same time makes us wonder whether we are getting anywhere in the long run. This is the way to spiritual exhaustion and burnout. This is the way to spiritual death.

Well, you and I don't have to kill ourselves. We are Beloved. We are intimately loved long before our parents, teachers, spouses, children and friends loved or wounded us. That's the truth of our lives. That's the truth I want you to claim for yourself. That's the truth spoken by the voice that says, 'You are my beloved.'

Listening to that voice with great inner attentiveness, I hear at my center words that say: 'I have called you by name, from the very beginning. You are mine and I am yours. You are my Beloved, on you my favor rests.' "

— from *Life of the Beloved* by Henri Nouwen

When we hear that we are the beloved, we remember that what we see and experience every day isn't the only thing that is real. Love is real. The love of the Father that proclaims, "You are my beloved," was real and at work in every moment of Jesus' life: his birth, baptism, transfiguration, death and resurrection. We claim this truth for ourselves as well. We are his beloved, from our birth to our death and every ordinary day in-between. We don't have to run after things that will only exhaust and disappoint us—we already have what we seek. We don't have to listen to all the words of criticism and negative that are spoken to us—we already have heard a better, truer word.

Have you claimed that truth for yourself? How might you hear God speaking, "You are my beloved," in your life today?

SATURDAY // DAY 70
READING :: Luke 9:28-36

Transfiguration always seems to be followed by difficulty and darkness. It's as if the higher we climb on the mountaintop, the further into darkness we descend on the other side. For a moment, we have glimpsed or tasted the beauty of the Kingdom, but we are soon reminded of our broken and bent world.

Maybe this is not such a bad thing. Instead of feeling disillusioned when we encounter darkness in or around us, one of the best things we can do is to take some simple steps to live as Kingdom people. To live as people who participate in the Kingdom of God breaking into our present age in big and small ways. We see, experience and participate in the in-breaking of the Kingdom every time we care for the sick, sit with the lonely, lift up the poor and broker peace.

Don't make the highs what you live for. Don't numb or distract yourself from the problems around you. Instead, let's become a people who help answer the prayer "Thy kingdom come, Thy will be done" in all our ordinary moments. This requires living a new kind of reality, one we caught a glimpse of on the mountain and now bring crashing into our everyday lives.

Meditation ::.

"The world around us tells us that life is about money, security, power, success. Yet the Gospels tell us that life is about something completely other. Real life, the Gospels tell us, is about doing the will of God, speaking for the poor, changing the lives of widows and orphans, exalting the status of women, refusing to make war, laying down our lives for the other, the invisible, and the enemy. It is about taking everyone in instead of leaving anyone out."

— from *The Liturgical Year: The Spiraling Adventure of the Spiritual Life*
by Joan Chittister

What is your response to the darkness and difficulty you face in your ordinary life? Do you shrink back and look for distraction, or do you figure out how to help the Kingdom break in?

NOW

ORDINARY TIME :: SUNDAY #11

2 Samuel 18:5-9, 15, 31-33
Psalm 130

Ephesians 4:25-5:2
John 6:35, 41-51

Has a teacher ever yelled at you, "No running in the hallways"? Or has a parent ever admonished you, "Walk, don't run"? It's been a few years since this happened to me but now I say it to my kids. And from time to time, when I'm running from one thing to another and feeling especially stressed, a voice will come from somewhere in the recesses of my mind, whispering these words to me afresh, "Walk, don't run." It's as if the voice is saying, "Slow down. Take it in. There's no hurry."

During the season of Advent, before Christmas, we focus on the idea of waiting. We are reminded that when we find ourselves having to wait, God is able to fill our moments with purpose and even make them into a gift. We don't just wait when something is wrong or when we have somehow missed something. Advent allows us to learn to wait in the way of Jesus. During Ordinary Time, we learn a similar lesson—not necessarily to wait, but to just slow down, be present and live in the now.

Our culture lives a fast-paced, planned-out, running-around, freeway kind of life. I live in an area where I can drive five or ten minutes away and see wide open fields, full of cows and green grass. But in the middle of those wide-open fields, workers are beginning to build four- and six-lane roads. Do you know how many dirt roads I see being carved out in the countryside? That's right—none! Everybody seems to want to go faster, to get somewhere more exciting.

Where are you trying to "get"? Is the present just a pit-stop on the way to where you want to be? How much of now do you sacrifice with thoughts of how and when you are going to get to tomorrow?

During Ordinary Time, we all need to be encouraged to walk, not run. To pause and ask, "What beauty is right here in front of me?" While everybody around us is speeding up, maybe Christ followers need to live each day with an awareness and presence that sets an example in our hectic world. He offers us rest, not more rushing.

Do you think about tomorrow more than you do today? How could you slow down and take in the beauty around you right now?

91

Meditation ::.

"If we're ever going to experience the fullness of life that the New Testament promises us, we're going to have to tear down the walls that compartmentalize the spiritual and the normal. We're going to have to except a new definition of normal. And this means we need to get over our mistaken idea that the practice of the presence of God is only for the super holy. The call to practice the presence of God is not a hyper-spiritual exercise. On the contrary, it's the core of what it means to surrender our life to Christ. Though few realize it, this practice is woven into the very fabric of the New Testament, written for all followers of Jesus. Aspiring to remain awake to God's ever present love is simply an aspect, a foundational aspect of what C. S. Lewis referred to as 'mere Christianity.' "

— from *Present Perfect: Finding God in the Now* by Gregory Boyd

Much of the difference between those who claim a "spiritual life" and those who wouldn't is simply an awareness of God's presence. No matter how "spiritual" we consider ourselves to be, we all must learn this art of awareness. Seasons like Advent and Lent and Pentecost help foster this kind of awareness, but it's also crucial to focus on God's presence in Ordinary Time. Awareness to his presence with us and his enveloping love for us should be a very normal, everyday part of our lives.

Did you know you can sense God's presence during any average moment—from doing your homework to mowing the lawn? Brother Lawrence is the patron saint of this kind of awareness. He called it "practicing the presence of God." Brother Lawrence found that during his daily task of dish-washing in the monastery where he lived, he powerfully sensed the presence and love of God. What is a more ordinary task than washing dishes? Pay attention to these most ordinary moments and you might just find, like Jacob in our Scripture for today, "The Lord is in this place, and I was not aware of it."

What are some mundane activities you do every day, like brushing your teeth or putting on your shoes? Ask God to show you his presence in all those moments.

In our culture, it's a badge of honor to say, "I'm busy." We all try to prove to one other that we're the busiest and the most stressed, as if that's a desirable way to live. The Israelites in their Egyptian captivity were no different. They lived at a breakneck pace and had unreal production expectations. Even when they left Egypt and saw a different version of life, they struggled to break free and trust that the world didn't revolve around their efforts. It's in this narrative that God gifted them with the commandment of Sabbath-keeping. He wasn't trying to make them slaves to just another rule or god, but to actually free them to live the lives he had created them to live—one of fullness and abundance rather than fear and scarcity.

Sabbath was and is a totally different version of living. By requiring the Israelites to take one day out of the week to simply rest, trusting in his provision rather than in themselves, God subverts our crazy, busy, running-around lives even today. Sabbath teaches us to live differently every day of the week not just one day of the week.

If you're the church-going type, the Sabbath-keeping kind of person, you know what I'm talking about. We try and worship on the Sabbath, we connect with our community, we pray—thanking God and asking God for guidance—we take communion, we remember what Jesus has done for us. On the Sabbath we do other things too, like confess our sins, open our Bibles and recite our beliefs. Let's be honest, these are all things that we benefit from in everyday life, not just Sunday life.

Walter Brueggemann in his book *Sabbath as Resistance: Saying No to the Culture of Now* says, "Moses, in Deuteronomy, imagines that Sabbath is not only a festival day but also a new social reality that is carried back into days one through six. People who keep Sabbath live all seven days differently."

> When is the last time you took a Sabbath? What would happen if you stopped the frantic pace of life to rest in God's provision for you?

There is a famous quote attributed to St. Augustine, "Our hearts are restless until they rest in you, O God."

I can attest to the truth of this statement. Not only in the "I once was restless and then I became a Christian" kind of way but in the everyday, ordinary moments of life. I get so excited about where God is leading me tomorrow that I fail to rest in his presence today. I always act as if God will be *there*—in that place or space he is calling me to go—forgetting that he is present to me here and has something for me *now*.

In today's reading, God tells Moses, "Come up to me on the mountain and stay here …" It's as if he is saying, "Come up on the mountain and be on the mountain! Don't worry about the past and its difficulties. Don't think about the future—how you'll get down the mountain or how you'll lead those people. Right now, this moment is the only thing that is real, and you need to just stay here, in my love and presence."

Living in the past or the future is a struggle for all of us. But today is the Day the Lord has made, and we should rejoice and be glad in it (Psalm 118:24).

So take a moment right now and rest.

Not only in the fact that you are saved by grace through faith, as a gift from the Creator God. But because this Creator God is also present and active right here and now. He offers you rest right now. *Be here, stay here.* And may the peace of the Lord be with you.

> Do you ever find yourself restless? Will you take a deep breath
> and rest in God today?

Meditation ::.

"Best of any song
is bird song
in the quiet, but first
you must have the quiet."

— from *This Day: Collected & New Sabbath Poems* by Wendell Berry

Each season of the church year is a gift that offers us particular aspects of abundant life. In Ordinary Time, there is a lot of quiet. That's a gift. Even when it seems empty, boring or like nothing is really happening, the quiet is a gift from God, who gives all gifts in their right season.

We are tempted to think that Ordinary Time is dull. But ordinary does not equal dull. May we not forget that every ordinary moment is dripping with God's divine presence. That quiet enables us to hear the beauty of a bird song and maybe the whisper of God's ever-present love and grace.

Receive the gift of quiet. Be joyful in these quiet moments. Learn to relax, rest and listen as one who is constantly being shaped and formed into the image of God.

Are you tempted to view quiet space as empty instead of full? The next time you have a quiet moment, will you tune your ears to hear?

I recently saw a picture on Facebook. A fellow was on a boat, presumably whale-watching. He was sitting down on the edge of the bow, looking at his phone, while a huge humpback whale was coming up for air just inches from his boat. The hashtag read: "Missed it."

I have a confession: I am that guy all too often. I am looking at my phone instead of that smile on my sons' faces or that glint in my daughter's eye. My guess is that you're that person from time to time as well—missing what's right in front of you because you're on your phone, buried in a book, hiding behind a camera, or just focusing on tomorrow.

I talk a lot about spiritual disciplines and silent retreats not because these disciplines or the practice of silence is how I am naturally wired. It's actually the exact opposite. I really struggle to be a disciplined person, to pray and read my Bible every day is a challenge not to mention the weightier spiritual disciplines. I'm drawn to the spiritual disciplines not because it all comes easy to me but rather because my formation into Christlikeness is important to me and I need these disciplines in my life to pursue that value, to help me to be more like Christ. And silence … forget about it. Half of the reason I jump on my phone or open my computer isn't to simply be productive but it's to fill the empty, ordinary space with something more exciting. Silence is often more uncomfortable than it is transcendent. Especially when you first try and enter it.

I need to look up. Be present. See what's God's doing all around me. Hurry less, walk more. Slow down and take it in. Not because that sounds so fun and easy, but because it is necessary and important for my soul. It might not come naturally but we must learn the unforced rhythm of grace and accept him as our refuge.

Have you ever missed something awesome because you were on your phone or hurrying to your next thing? Are you willing to limit your time on your phone or electronics to be more present to those around you and to me more present to God?

FOLLOW

1 Kings 2:10-12, 3:3-14 | Ephesians 5:15-20
Psalm 111 | John 6:51-58

If you've been a Christian for any amount of time, the idea of "following Jesus" isn't new to you. But during Ordinary Time, we have a chance to understand more about what it means to follow him each day, to accept his call no matter what. It may not be flashy or fun, but it's the only way we can experience abundant life. This week is another opportunity to learn what should be true about all of us: We follow Jesus.

Meditation ::.

"If the Son of Man is the King of this world, we who worship him are to follow him, and are therefore sent into the world with a great commission. We are to make disciples, learners, followers; we are to baptize them, and teach them to observe all that Jesus commanded. There is no corner of the created universe over which Jesus does not claim rightful sovereignty. We are to be his agents, his ambassadors, in bringing the word of his Kingdom to all his subjects. The coronation anthem contains a line of music for every creature, and the harmony will not be complete until they all join in."

— from *Following Jesus: Biblical Reflections on Discipleship*
by N. T. Wright

Prayer on the Call of Christ
Lord Jesus Christ, I hear your call.
I want to accept it and walk with you.
I do not know what in me might move you to select me to walk among your friends.
It does not matter. You have chosen me. I accept.
Here in your presence and with all my heart, I say:
> "To my Lord I give
> the hours of my life
> and the use of my death."
Now, Lord, keep me your own before the Father.
Nothing matters more to me than that. Amen.

— from *The Montserrat Jesuit Retreat House Prayer Book*

What would an average day in your life look like if you truly followed Jesus?

If you could have breakfast with one living person, who would it be? For me it would be N. T. Wright, Jimmy Fallon or maybe Bono. With each of them, I can close my eyes and imagine the conversation, the laughs we would have and the friendship we would forge. Each of these breakfasts would end the same way, with them saying, "This was the best breakfast I have had in a long time. You should come follow me. Be my teacher's assistant / co-host / backup guitar player." Hey, a guy can dream, right?

St. Ignatius of Loyola suggests you imagine this very scenario as a spiritual exercise. First, imagine having breakfast with a modern-day hero or heroine. Then imagine this person coming on the scene, how impressed and amazed you would be as the person passed you by. Finally, imagine that just before this hero walked past, he or she looked straight at you and said, "Come follow me." How would you feel? What would you say?

Now, imagine King Jesus coming on the scene. Put yourself in the story you read today in Matthew 4. But instead of Jesus looking at Peter, he looks at you and says, "Come follow me." How would you feel? What would you say?

Ignatius says that of course you would follow Jesus even more than an earthly king. But he reminds the participant that following Jesus means following him in the good and the bad. It means following him in ALL he says and does. Ignatius says this:

"Without doubt I am unworthy to march after Thee; but full of confidence in Thy grace and protection, I consecrate myself to Thee without reserve. All that I am and all that I possess I submit to Thy holy will. I declare … my desire, my unalterable resolution, my determined will is to fill Thee as nearly as possible …"

Spend some time today imagining these scenarios. Are you more excited to follow Jesus than anyone else? Are you willing to pray the same prayer as Ignatius?

Have you ever heard the phrase "covered in the dust of the rabbi"? I first heard it from the high school teacher and Holy Land expert Ray Vander Laan. In talking about the Jewish concept of discipleship, Ray explains how a rabbi would invite only the best Torah/Bible students to follow him and be his disciples. These disciples expected that they would follow their rabbi so closely that at the end of a long day, after walking around the ancient world of dirt roads and dusty paths, they would be covered in all the dirt and dust their rabbi had kicked up. What a powerful idea: following your rabbi so closely that whatever they have gotten into would be all over you as well.

As we follow Jesus, our rabbi, we need to ask, "What is Jesus getting into?" Do we find ourselves covered in that same dust?

For instance, Jesus seemed to always be mixing it up with the hurting and marginalized, the have-nots. Are we covered in the dust of a life shared with folks nobody else wants to be around, especially not good "religious" folks?

Jesus always seemed to be forgiving people and offering them not only seven second chances, but 77 second chances. Are we covered in the dust of love and forgiveness, even when it's undeserved or at our own expense?

Jesus always seemed to be healing the sick and helping the blind to see. In our passage for today these are the things Jesus points to in order to help John understand who he is and that he is worth following.

Are we covered in the dust of bringing light, life and healing to a sorrowful and broken world? Are we shining light into the kinds of dark places Jesus always sought out?

If we don't notice any of Jesus' dust on us, maybe we need to follow him more closely.

> Are you covered with the dust Jesus leaves behind? If not, how can you get closer to him?

This idea of following Jesus moves us from merely knowing about Jesus to actually knowing him personally—so well, in fact, that you go where he goes and do what he does.

When I was looking at seminaries to attend, I considered a school with a great divinity program that has produced some amazing biblical and theological minds. I was really encouraged until I learned that the professor of New Testament studies wasn't a Christian. If I enrolled at this school, the Bible classes I would take would be informational and academic but nothing more.

I am positive I could have learned a lot of great information about Jesus in those Bible classes. But there would have been no way for that professor to actually help me know Jesus more. My goal for graduate school was not just to get smarter but to learn to follow Jesus well so that I could help others to follow him well. I didn't want to just know about Jesus. I needed to *know* Jesus.

Meditation ::.

"We cannot grasp Christ merely with our heads or our hearts. We come to understand him through a total, all-embracing practice of living; and that means discipleship. In the Reformation period, the Anabaptist Hans Denk put it by saying: 'No one is able verily to know Christ except he follow him in life.' Discipleship is the holistic knowledge of Christ, and for the people involved it has a cognitive as well as an ethical relevance: it means knowing and doing both."

— from *Jesus Christ for Today's World* by Jürgen Moltmann

Do you ever feel like you're just trying to learn more about Jesus? How can you shift your focus to actually *knowing* Jesus?

Author Søren Kierkegaard lived in a time when Christianity was the dominant and government-supported religion of the day. Never one to conform, Kierkegaard raised some very unpopular questions, such as, "If everybody is a Christian, is anybody really a Christian?" He was challenging the misconception that you can be born into Christianity or simply live in a Christian nation and therefore be a Christian. Kierkegaard proposed that one must resign all else and take a leap of faith to follow Christ and claim the title of Christian. To be a Christian will cost you something and will take you many places you may not wish to go. But to go is to be a Christian, to follow is to be holy, and to pray is to say yes.

With this in mind, we let Kierkegaard encourage and then pray for us.

Meditation ::.

"It does not say that you should try to resemble Christ. No, you are to put on Christ, put him on yourself—as when someone goes around in borrowed clothing—put him on, as when someone who looks strikingly like another not only tries to resemble him but represents him. Christ gives you this clothing (the satisfaction of atonement) so that you might represent him."

— from *Provocations; Spiritual Writing of Kierkegaard*
edited by Charles E. Moore

Prayer ::.

O Lord Jesus Christ, You did not come to the world to be served, but also surely not to be admired or in that sense to be worshipped. You are the way and the truth and it was only followers you demanded. Awake us therefore if we have dozed away into this delusion, save us from the error of wishing to admire you instead of being willing to follow you and resemble you.

— from *The Prayers of Kierkegaard* edited by Perry D. LeFevre

When is the last time you followed Jesus into a place
you did not wish to go?

In our culture, there seems to be many ways to get what you want. Some will get you there faster. Some will get you there with a cleaner conscience or with friends and family by your side. But there are a lot of ways to get there, right? Wherever your "there" might be.

I had a friend in college who sold cutlery for a summer. I was one of his first pitches. I remember him cutting a penny in half and sawing through a soda can, and proclaiming that these knives were the only way to go. Nothing else could even compare. I didn't buy a knife that summer, but they sure were cool!

Lots of people believe their favorite "this" or favorite "that" is so much better than all the other options. But no matter what your goal is, following Jesus is the best way to get there, maybe even only way. You could manipulate yourself to some kind of success; you could work your fingers to the bone for a bank account full of money; you could even wear all the right clothes or do all the right things to get people to like you. But the only way to really get what your soul longs for is to follow Jesus. When life is hard, when suffering hits, when things don't add up and nothing seems to make sense, Jesus has paved the way ahead for you. If you will follow him, you are sure to get where you ultimately want to go. Even better, you will get where he wants you to go.

Meditation ::.

"Jesus, the Son of God, the truly human one, is leading his people to their promised land, and is available for all people and for all time as the totally sympathetic one, the priest through who they can come to God. Following Jesus is the only way to go."

— from *Following Jesus: Biblical Reflections on Discipleship*
by N. T. Wright

Do you trust that following Jesus is absolutely the
only way to truly live life?

POINTING

ORDINARY TIME :: SUNDAY #13

1 Kings 8:1, 6, 10-11, | Ephesians 6:10-20
22-30, 41-43 | John 6:56-69
Psalm 84 |

There is a short video on my phone where I am begging my son to sing "Jesus Loves Me." Instead, he continues to bust into the "ABC's" song. Every time I watch that video it reminds me of the amazing moment when I first heard Jack sing, "Jesus loves me, this I know, for the Bible tells me so." I don't delete that video because it didn't capture the exact moment I wanted. Rather, I save it because that image points me to what I do want to remember. It points me to all the love and beauty that my son has given me, and ultimately it fills me with gratitude to God, the giver of the gift.

God is always giving us these sorts of images and icons that point us, ultimately, to himself. He gives us all kinds of things that point to a greater reality just beyond what we can actually see—the reality of his love and his Kingdom at work. We can't fully capture it with our phones or cameras, but all the beauty God has created points to him. It's all an icon. No art, religious image or beautiful sunset can fully show us what God looks like or how he loves, but in these ordinary, everyday things, we can catch a glimpse of the divine. Once we are pointed beyond the created thing to the Creator, our response will be worship. We lift our voice and open our hearts in gratitude for the goodness and beauty that only God can give us.

Meditation ::.

"Regard for creation urges us to the Creator who we address in wonder, awe, amazement, and gratitude. The ultimate expression of our attentiveness, the conclusion drawn, does not lead to a scientific formulation, to an intellectual conclusion, or to technical certainty, but to lyrical self-abandonment. Such attentiveness leads finally to doxology, to the ceding of life in its wonder and gratitude over to the one who is it progenitor, sponsor, and sovereign."

— from *Remember You Are Dust* by Walter Brueggemann

Take a walk today. Notice this divine presence in what you see and touch and taste and hear. Give thanks to God that his love is evident, revealed all around you and to pointing you to himself.

It's incredible how ordinary, everyday things reveal and point to a divine Creator. In a song, a painting or a mountain range, we see glimpses of God and his creative love and divine Kingdom at work. But when and why does our view go wrong? We've all experienced an image that we probably shouldn't have seen and now it's burned into our memory or some other image that does anything but point us to God. The Bible has a term for all the things that fail to point to the Creator God: *idol*. An idol is a failed icon, something that has failed to point to the Creator and instead takes that which belongs to God—trust, belief, love, worship, etc.—and keeps those things for itself. An idol finds its end in the created instead of the Creator.

Unfortunately, we're the ones who give created things this power. We turn what is good and beautiful into idols and seek our fulfillment in them. Paul says in our reading for today that an idol isn't really anything at all. He's even more direct in 1 Corinthians 8:4, "We know that 'an idol is nothing at all in the world' and that 'there is no God but one.' "

What ordinary things do you let keep you from God? Created things can either evoke our worship of Jesus or steal it. For example, we are all tempted to worship at the altar of acceptance and love, safety and security, or wisdom and reason; but these idols are nothing but golden calves. Your spouse or children, your work or bank account, even your pastor and church were never meant to give you ultimate fulfillment but instead to point you to the only one who actually gives that ultimate, abundant fulfillment: Jesus.

Meditation ::.

"John Calvin famously said that all our hearts are idol-making factories. He understood how all of us are drawn down this idolatry track every day, Christian people and non-Christian people, in-church people and out-of-church people. We habitually look to something or someone smaller than Jesus for the things we crave and need."

— from *Jesus + Nothing = Everything* by Tullian Tchividjian

Get quiet before the Lord, spend a moment in worship, then ask him, "Is there anything I am making an idol, that I am worshiping other than you?"

Meditation ::.

"The question is not what we intended ourselves to be, but what he intended us to be when he made us. He is the inventor, we are only the machine. He is the painter, we are only the picture. How should we know what he means us to be like? ... We may be content to remain what we call 'ordinary people': but he is determined to carry out a quite different plan. To shrink back from that plan is not humility: it is laziness and cowardice. To submit to it is not conceit or megalomania: it is obedience ... No possible degree of holiness or heroism which has ever been recorded of the greatest saints is beyond what he is determined to produce in every one of us in the end. The job will not be completed in this life: but he means to get us as far as possible before death."

— from *C. S. Lewis: Readings for Meditation and Reflection*
edited by Walter Hooper

Jesus' life was the example of the life we are called to live. His eating and sleeping, walking and talking was all meant to point us to a life that is authentically human—the life we are called to live. Jesus came for many important reasons, and showing us how to be the best kind of human was one of them.

Time and time again, Jesus showed us what it looks like to be connected to the Father (John 17:21), work with the Father (John 5:17), and do what the Father wants at every turn (John 4:34). If we want to live a life of abundance, the most authentically human life, all we have to do is look at Jesus.

Often we lift up other icons of the life we wish to live. But are the people we view as icons pointing us to the greatest realities and the best kind of life? Jesus is the only perfect image that will truly lead us to the life we were created to live—fully connected to God, our creator and sustainer.

Who or what do you lift up as the icons of the life you wish you could live? What do these icons point you to?

THURSDAY // DAY 89
READING :: Matthew 6:1-18

Do you ever try to pray like Jesus teaches in Matthew 6:6? The get-alone, get-quiet, close-the-door, talk-to-your-Heavenly Father, just-you-and-him kind of prayer? Do you find it hard to do? Yeah, me too!

A few years ago, I became fascinated with Christian icons. You may have noticed I post them on the Web Guide sometimes. Christian icons are images that point us to the greater meaning of the people, places and stories depicted in the Bible. They give us a visual of spiritual realities. Unlike a normal picture or painting, Christian icons are not trying to accurately or realistically depict a person or scene. They're trying to lead the one who gazes upon the image into prayer and thought about the deeper things of God.

Icons help me to focus in prayer and in life. They help to keep my eyes fixed on Jesus and my life pointed in his direction. Icons help push out all the negative and distracting images that occupy my head and heart. I try to let an image of Jesus push out ones of greed or sex or judgment. My desire for you and me is that while we're praying, our minds would be filled with images of Jesus and his story of love and redemption. Icons have helped this to be accomplished in my prayer and in my life.

Meditation ::.

"Over the centuries, icons have been described in many ways. They've been called hymns, sermons, prayers clothed with color, images of faith, pictorial theology, windows into heaven, and the Gospels proclaimed in visual form. I invite you to consider that icons are tangible affirmations of the Incarnation that offer us moments of sacramental encounter with the Source of all holiness. Incarnational faith proclaims that God has entered into our reality by becoming a human person in Jesus of Nazareth. Because of this, all created things are hallowed by God's presence and possess the potential to speak to us of their creator. Christian faith hinges on a belief in the Incarnation—for us God has a human face."

— from *A Brush with God* by Peter Pearson

What images fill your mind and imagination? Could an image of Jesus help point you to him in prayer today?

John the Baptist is one of the best biblical examples of a living icon. John's whole life was lived with a single purpose, to point people to Jesus. Everything he did, said, ate, wore, yelled and argued was meant to point to Jesus, the coming Messiah, and the Kingdom he was bringing. All the attention he got—and John would have drawn some eyes—was meant to be simultaneously reflected for the purpose of proclaiming the King and his Kingdom!

How often do we try to draw attention to ourselves—for our own sake? It's human nature to walk away from getting a pat on the back and saying, "Yeah, I am kind of awesome!" That's why we call it American Idol, not American Icon. Each of the contestants wants to acquire fame; they want to be worshiped and adored and have no real goal of pointing to anything beyond themselves.

Though our culture strives for fame, some men and woman do the opposite. Martin Luther King Jr., was a modern-day icon. He lived for something beyond himself. He lived in such a way that it cost him and his family. Even more than equality and racial justice, he lived for God and his Kingdom to be made known and manifest on earth as it is in heaven. MLK lived his life pointing to God and his Kingdom even at the expense of his own life.

I could go on to describe others like St. Francis or St. Ignatius, Willam Wilberforce and Mother Teresa who also lived in such a way that they pointed to Jesus with every breath they took. But I'm sure you see that ordinary men and women can be living, breathing images of God's love and goodness, reflecting attention away from themselves and toward the one they follow, Jesus.

> "Yes, Lord, walking in the way of your law, we wait for you;
> your name and renown are the desire of our hears (Isaiah 26:8)."

Who have you witnessed living in such a way that they make Jesus, not themselves famous? Identify their characteristics and ask God to give you the strength, courage and humility to imitate them as they follow Christ.

Meditation ::.

"All of life is to be lived cora Deo, they said—that is, before the face of God. All vocations can be holy, for all of our cultural labors can be expressions of tending God's world. There is no 'secular' because there is no square inch of creation that is not the Lord's.

The result is what Taylor calls 'sanctification of ordinary life.' On the one hand, this has a leveling effect: the monk is no holier than the farmer, the nun no holier than the mother. Renunciation is no longer seen as the shortcut to divine blessing; if anything, it is seen as perhaps spurning God's good gifts. On the other hand, it's not just that the renunciative vocations are laid low; on the contrary, the expectations are ratcheted up for lay people. Engagement in domestic life is no longer a free pass from pursuing holiness. So while ordinary, domestic life is taken up and sanctified, renunciation is now built into ordinary life. So the butcher, the baker, and the candlestick maker are affirmed in their 'worldly' stations as also called to serve God, just like the priest ..."

— from *Discipleship in the Present Tense* by James K. A. Smith

During Ordinary Time, we realize that all of life, even the most monotonous or the most ordinary parts, are filled with divine energy and life. God—Father, Son and Holy Spirit—is present in every place and every time.

We are called to live *cora Deo*, before the face of God. We are called to holiness. Every single person is an image-bearer of the one true God. On the path of our everyday, ordinary lives, we experience the wind of God and help others do the same.

This "sanctification of ordinary life" is exactly what Ordinary Time is all about. During Ordinary Time, we have learned to live lives that, every day in every way, point to Jesus, what he is doing and what he—Father, Son and Holy Spirit—will ultimately do.

WHAT'S NEXT

The goal of Ordinary Time is to learn how to follow Jesus in everyday, ordinary life. If you've made it through this book and are keeping track of the liturgical calendar, you're halfway there! Hopefully these first thirteen weeks of Ordinary Time will be a springboard into the second half of Ordinary Time. Hopefully this first half will help you to live every ordinary day well, with your eyes fixed on Jesus, the author and perfecter of your faith. Pick up a Bible and a book and spend the rest of Ordinary Time learning to follow Jesus in an ordinary everyday way. Check out the Web Guide for a few recommendations.

Also, Advent is the next season on the liturgical calendar. It follows Ordinary Time but actually begins the liturgical year. Pick up a copy of my *Advent* devotional and continue to be shaped by the story of Jesus, which is lived through the liturgical calendar.

"As I worked my way into adulthood I was reading my Bible with more diligence, paying attention to how this gospel of Jesus got lived, not just talked about, not just given witnessed to, not just studied and memorized. I gradually realized that ordinary time is not what biblical people endure or put up with or hurry through as we wait around for the end time and its rocket launch into eternity. It is a gift through which we participate in the present and daily work of God. I finally got it, end time influences present ordinary time, not by diminishing or denigrating it but by charging it, filing it with purpose and significance. The end time is not a future we wait for but the gift of the fullness of time that we receive in adoration and obedience as it flows into the present."

— from *Christ Plays in Ten Thousand Places* by Eugene Peterson

web : www.erikwillits.com
blog : ww.erikwillitsblog.com
email : erik@erikwillits.com
twitter : twitter.com/erikwillits
facebook : facebook.com/erikwillits
instagram : erikwillits